PENGUIN BOOKS
BBC BOOKS

TERRIBLE PETS

Sarah Kennedy, a former speech and drama teacher, made the move into television and radio. Her wide experience ranges from the Saturday night hit show *Game for a Laugh* to programmes covering the arts, current affairs and travel; and from the wedding of the Duke and Duchess of York to the twenty-four-hour British Telethon. She is currently working with Dr Desmond Morris on the *Animal Country* series, which is now in its ninth year. Her awards include Female Personality of the Year, for ITV in 1982 and for the BBC in 1984; TV Woman of the Year, awarded by the Variety Club of Great Britain, in 1984; and the 1995 Sony Breakfast Show Award for *Dawn Patrol*, her programme on BBC Radio Two.

Sarah Kennedy loves gardening, Shakespeare and cooking. Humour is a very important ingredient in her life and work. In 1995 the first edition of *The Terrible Twos*, now available in Penguin, reached the top of the bestsellers list, raising £100,000 for BBC's Children In Need. In 1996 the follow-up hardback edition of *Terrible Pets* went straight to No. 1 in the bestsellers list, raising funds for the People's Dispensary for Sick Animals (PDSA). Sarah is currently writing her first novel, due to be published in Easter 1997.

Terrible Pets

Compiled by
SARAH KENNEDY

PENGUIN BOOKS
BBC BOOKS

PENGUIN BOOKS

BBC BOOKS

Published by the Penguin Group
Penguin Books Ltd, 27 Wrights Lane, London w8 5tz, England
Penguin Books USA Inc., 375 Hudson Street, New York, New York 10014, USA
Penguin Books Australia Ltd, Ringwood, Victoria, Australia
Penguin Books Canada Ltd, 10 Alcorn Avenue, Toronto, Ontario, Canada m4v 3b2
Penguin Books (NZ) Ltd, 182–190 Wairau Road, Auckland 10, New Zealand

Penguin Books Ltd, Registered Offices: Harmondsworth, Middlesex, England

First published by BBC Books, a division of BBC Worldwide Ltd 1996
This expanded edition published in Penguin Books 1996
10 9 8 7 6 5 4 3 2 1

Typeset in 10.5/12.75pt Monotype Bembo by
Rowland Phototypesetting Ltd, Bury St Edmunds, Suffolk
Printed in England by Clays Ltd, St Ives plc

Contents

Preface

Dawn patrollers are well known in BBC Radio 2 for writing simply brilliant letters. I throw out a talking point, and you lot are off like greyhounds after the rabbit. This reminds me of the *The Terrible Twos* tale: toddler watching dog-racing on TV rushes into the kitchen, saying – 'Mum, mum, some doggies on TV were chasing a rabbit and the rabbit won'.

After the amazing success of *The Terrible Twos* raising a large amount of money for BBC Children In Need, I never planned a second book. It just happened; and, once again, it's *OUR* book. A listener wrote: 'YOU couldn't have done it without US and we couldn't have done it without YOU'.

This book, then, is a small thank-you for all the enormous pleasure, company, fun and love our pets give us.

Why *Terrible Pets*? I think it all started with my aged Ps. My mother, the Beatific Mary, left on top of the fridge a tranquillizer wedged in a piece of Cheddar. This was for McGregor, a yellow Labrador pup, who hated cars. The vet prescribed the pills, mother produced the cheese, Father – hungry for his lunch – picked up the morsel and the rest is family history. McGregor bounced and woofed up and down on the back seat; Father, with nice wet nose, started to fall asleep at the wheel!

As soon as I told this tale on *Dawn Patrol*, the mail flood-gates opened. In poured absolutely hilarious tales of terrible pets.

I was then introduced to Heather Cary. She's done our cartoons; and Barbara Nash has again put her editorial stamp on *Terrible Pets*, just as she did on *The Terrible Twos*. In fact, the monster on my lap is Barbara's pup, Bertie – the naughtiest of the litter!

As I write this, *Terrible Pets* has been in the Bestsellers Hardback list for three months benefiting the People's Dispensary for Sick Animals (PDSA) and pet stories are still a major feature of my postbag. Standby for *Terrible Howlers*?

In the meantime I have spent 1996 writing my first novel. Now I hope you are not thinking 'Terrible Novel' . . .

Sarah Kennedy

PS: Some of the letters in this book are a timely reminder that cans, cartons and jars can be dangerous for small animals.

Woofs

Dear Sarah,
*Please please help me. I'm writing to you because I know you
are kind to dumb animals. My name is Barney Murphy. I am
a rather large six-year-old Dalmatian and I live with my family,
Rona, Tony and their two daughters Helen and Susan.*

*Helen is getting married to Martin Willoughby and, as you
can imagine, everybody is very excited and looking forward to
the Big Day. However, I heard them talking, when they thought
I was asleep, and, shock of shocks, I am **not** being invited.
There is some pathetic excuse that I get excited, jump up at
people, sometimes knock them over, lick their faces and ears etc.,
etc.*

*I don't understand – when will they realize that getting
excited, jumping up, licking people's faces and ears is what I do.
I'm a dog for goodness' sake, not a brain surgeon – one despairs
of humans sometimes! Anyhow, as a result I am being sent to
kennels for a few days. I expect they will tell me I am going on
holiday, which is what they usually say. This means I will not
be here on the Big Day and I am really disappointed. I was so
looking forward to seeing all the family, posing for the photographs
and generally making a nuisance of myself, but it's not to be.*

*The worst thing is that I won't be there to give Helen and
Martin my love and best wishes.*

I was at a complete loss until I thought of you. I know you *love animals from watching you on TV's **Animal Country** with Mr Desmond Morris and listening to you each morning on the radio with all your funny stories, especially the ones about dogs.*

So I am writing to ask you if you would please be kind enough to let people know how dogs feel about these things, and if you can also wish Helen and Martin all the best on the Big Day.

I will be ever so grateful and, if we meet some day, I promise not to knock you over but I will probably lick your ears.

    Barney Murphy

Tea for . . . one more?

Janet and Bob were expecting friends for tea. In mid-afternoon they arrived, along with Boxer dog. House-proud Janet thought bringing the dog along was a bit of a cheek, and did not relish the thought of dog-hair all over her carpet, but she politely gritted her teeth and held her tongue even when the dog jumped up on the settee and slobbered for titbits. When dinner was served the dog followed, insisting on visiting everybody in turn for scraps from the table, then settled back on the settee again while coffee was served.

'You certainly spoil your dog,' one of the friends said suddenly to Janet.

'*My* dog!' Janet replied, nearly choking. 'You mean, *your* dog . . .'

'No,' said the friend, 'it arrived on the doorstep the same time as us.'

Exit Boxer followed by some unrepeatable words!

Maggie Foord

Toy boy

My four-year-old granddaughter was heart-broken at the death of the first dog she had ever loved. We both cried together and then talked it through in-depth with me struggling to come up with the appropriate answers to her life-and-death questions.

She finally dried her tears, thought for a moment, then said matter-of-factly: 'Can we stuff his body, so I can have him as a toy?'

She had obviously just remembered a museum visit.

Barbara Clarke

Return to sender . . .

Like most Labradors, my parents' golden Labrador, Boo, loved helping by carrying things around, anything from eggs from the hen-house, to an innocent passer-by's gloves. Boo could teach Fagin a thing or two about pick-pocketing.

Anyway, living in the country, as my parents do, it was about a mile to the nearest postbox, and, having an important letter which needed to be posted, my dad, then in his seventies, set out with Boo to post the letter. At the letter-box the postman was just getting into his van having emptied the box. He rolled down his window to take the letter from my dad.

Before either man knew what was happening Boo had

taken the letter from the postman's hand, and was happily
trotting towards home, tail wagging wildly. (Collecting the
post in the morning at the gate was a recently acquired party
trick.) Naturally she ignored all calls to stop, come back, or
anything else my Dad could think of to shout at her. Why
is it dogs get a convenient deafness when they want to?

Anyway, when he eventually arrived home, Dad found
a triumphant beaming Boo waiting on the doorstep, soggy
letter still in her mouth. How could anyone be cross with
such a helpful friend! The letter somehow lost its impor-
tance and waited until the next day when it had dried out.

Judith Twyman

Sock-it-to-them, Emma

Emma, our dotty Dobermann bitch, was born a glutton,
able to swallow anything in micro-seconds. One of her
more revolting 'fancies' – she was obviously still hungry
after her breakfast – emerged when we were walking along
a grassy cliff edge by a beach at Lee-on-Solent. Despite
all our cries, she constantly rushed off, zig-zagging her fat
ungainly body up and down the crowded beach where
people lay, bodies stripped off, by their bundles of clothes.

Soon, from the sudden activity of the sun-bathers and
swimmers, it became clear that she was grabbing guarded
and unguarded bundles of clothing, tossing them about,
making her selection and running off. By the time she
reached us, hotly pursued by several irate men, she looked
even more swollen than usual, but only had one item
trailing from her mouth.

We were not, however, left in the dark for long – she

had visited each bundle in turn and cleared the beach of dirty socks. Needless to say, while we dealt with the rumpus from the ex-sock-owners, she swallowed the evidence and beat a rapid retreat.

Ian C. Roberts

Requiem for innocence

I wrote the following poem when I had to have my first Sheep Dog put down – a *horrid* expression – when she was sixteen years old. She was given to me as a pup – as a welcoming present from a neighbouring farmer – when I moved to Devon from Birmingham to start farming. So, we both learned 'how' together and this added poignancy when I lost her.

The poem is taken from my first book, *Requiem for Innocence*, and I had a lot of 'phone calls from people who were 'touched' by it, including one from a person who was: 'Pleasantly surprised that a farmer could write such a sympathetic poem about an animal' . . . !

Sheep dog passing

He said, 'You needn't wait
if you'd rather' and called the nurse.
'It's for the best,' He said.

Whose best I'd like to know. It's
all very well for Him,
all glass and stainless steel.
'It will be quick,' He said

and filled the syringe.
'There will be no pain,' He said
and clipped the hair above the vein.

Holding her, she licked my hand and
understood: anything would be a piece of cake
after nights of blizzards on the moors
to pinpoint buried sheep, and rescue lambs
or, to a whistle, in the noontide heat
outrun, collect and fetch far flocks
from hills to lusher grounds.
Her eyes reminded me of little things, shared
times to treasure garnered over half a life.

'It's done,' He said
and dropped the needle in the stainless bowl.
At peace she watched me, sighed and slept.

Him in his glass and stainless world
said there would be no pain;
but he was wrong.

R. A. Chesterfield

What a good boy, am I!

Mick, our dog, it has to be said, is a naughty but obedient
dog. He persists in investigating the contents of carrier bags
when I arrive home from the supermarket, but obligingly
responds to my commands. Hearing him at it, while I was
trafficking carrier bags to and from the car, I shouted:
'*Drop it*'.

He did . . . at once to do him justice. *It* was a box of eggs. And, to add insult to injury, he trod and slithered all through the mess, as he came, tail down, to say sorry he had been caught with egg on his face.

Vicky Arscott

Follow that . . . deckchair
On holiday in Cornwall, we had to tether Herbie, our Yorkshire Terrier, to a deckchair because he kept pinching

the ball my husband and the boys were trying to play with. After watching their antics for a while, I decided to go for a paddle. So I piled the picnic things on to the deckchair and set off. I had just reached the water when there was a shout from the boys. I turned and there was Herbie towing the laden deckchair behind him determined at all costs not to be left behind. He looked like one of the contestants from the 'strongest man in the world'!

Hilary Nash

No parking

Returning to the car-park I saw, with a sinking heart, yet another traffic warden snapping her book shut and sticking a ticket to the windscreen of my car. Baffled and bewildered, I stood peering at the spot where I *knew* I had stuck the parking ticket. After a moment, angry with myself and none the wiser, convinced by now I was going bonkers, my eyes strayed from the windscreen to our Cocker Spaniel, Teddy, sitting on the front seat. Bored with waiting, he had taken the tickets and reparked them in his tummy.

I decided to pay the fine without even trying to explain.

Bobbin Eaglen

SK: Very wise, Bobbin.

What's in a name?

I was walking up the High Street when I noticed a stolid-looking infant dressed in a pixie hat and chunky coat waiting in his buggy. Tethered to the pushchair was a puppy, which began to wag all over as I approached.

'What's his name?' I asked the child.

'Bloody bugger,' came the dead-pan reply.

    Christine Hart

Cage to let

Our Irish Setter, Darrig, adored all small mammals, such as hamsters, guinea-pigs etc., (as have all my Setters), and used to gaze longingly at the guinea-pig in her raised cage.

One day I returned home to find the guinea-pig scuttling round our courtyard and was amazed to see that Darrig had opened the cage and had managed to squeeze inside, even squeezing himself through the small opening into the sleeping area. The whole cage was bursting with Setter. He was dozing happily and we had to dismantle the cage to get him out.

    Beryl Neighbour

Sex pest!

A few years ago we had a lovely Boxer, Nikki. One day as I was walking him along the promenade, he vanished into the long grass on Lovers' Hill. I thought he was chasing rabbits until I heard screams and shouts! Soon, Nikki appeared, grinning all over his face with a bra dangling from his teeth. He was so very pleased with himself, wagging his little stump of a tail and dancing back and forth, the bra swinging. I made several desperate grabs at it, but he thought it would be great fun to play tug-of-war.

Meanwhile, the disgruntled lovers were leaping around in the long grass, furious at having their passion interrupted, and the lady miffed at having her undies filched.

Nikki absolutely refused to relinquish his prize trophy and walked all the way home with it dangling from his jaws. He was delighted, whether with the bra, or the consternation he had caused, I was never quite sure.

Roxy Thompson

Just testing . . .
I had four G.S.Ds – three dogs and one bitch – and we had a purpose-designed dog-proof garden with a very secure wooden fence. One evening, however, there was a knock on the door. On opening it, I was confronted by my next-door neighbours' very irate daughter who informed me that her mother had been bitten by one of my dogs, and had just returned from hospital where she had received treatment. I really could not understand *how* she had been bitten as the garden was totally enclosed and dog-proof. So, I did no more, but flew round to my neighbours' house in a right old state, fearing the worst. On arrival, I was ushered into the front room where my neighbour, Molly, a very sweet Irish lady, was sitting nursing a finger with a very large bandage on it. She was a bit tearful, and I could not apologize enough for what had happened.

'Molly,' I said, 'please tell me, how did the dog bite your finger?'

'Well,' she said in her soft Irish brogue, 'I put my finger through one of those little knotholes in the fence, waggled it a bit just to see what would happen, and something bit me.'

To this day, I do not know how I kept a straight face! On return home, I went into the garden and proceeded to block up every small dog-height knothole in the fence. Which dog had bitten her, we never did know, but sometimes my sweet Misty used to stare rather wistfully at that fence, wondering, perhaps, if that sausage was going to appear again!

> *Ros Moore*

Murphy's law

We lived in a house that backed on to a major park and Murphy, our Irish Wolf Hound, because of his size and weight (fifteen-and-a-half stone!) used to take himself for a walk every day by simply walking straight through a large thorn hedge.

One day we were walking with him near some lakes, at the end of which was a small, high, narrow ice-cream caravan. Murphy suddenly ran ahead, skidded to a halt, sat down, and the ice-cream vendor unwrapped an ice-cream and threw it to him. Murphy swallowed this, without it even touching the sides of his mouth, got up, wagged his tail and came back to us. I went over to the ice-cream vendor to thank him and to offer to pay for the ice-cream, but he said: 'No, you don't have to. The dog and I have an arrangement. The first day we were here he smelt the ice-cream, jumped up, put a paw either side of the opening and the caravan nearly fell over under his weight. Now we give him an ice-cream, he doesn't push us over and the K-9 protection racket works well.'

We also had another dog – a black Labrador called Satan. Satan, unlike Murphy, did not relish ice-cream but he loved the cornet in which the ice-cream was contained. The dogs developed a double-act. Sometimes, Murphy took Satan with him. They would walk up behind some child waving a cornet around and neatly pluck the ice-cream out of the top. The child would look round and, seeing this huge shaggy animal, would scream and drop the cornet which Satan would pick up. So both were happy! It cost me a fortune in replacement ice-creams.

The third dog of the pack was a very small Jack Russell called Muppet. She was terrified of thunder and one day – at that stage my practice was at home – a patient was dropped off by taxi at the start of a thunder-storm. Muppet, frightened as usual and seeing an open door, fled, hopped into the taxi and settled down in the back.

The taxi driver apparently noticed her presence soon after, but for some reason failed to put two-and-two together. Instead of bringing her back to us, he took her to the police station. When we finally collected her we found that not only had he taken her to the police station, but he had charged for the taxi run. Her fear of thunder cost £3.50 – and she was told in future to go by bus!

One last Murphy story. We had some friends who stayed with us regularly. One, the husband, was a colleague of mine doing some training with me. Two, his wife, was a very petite American who, while being a great help at teaching the children to ride, was not very good at contributing to the general input of housework at the weekends, especially Sunday mornings.

One morning when everybody was at breakfast and she had not arrived, her husband Rick said 'Well, let's start without her'. We finished our breakfast and were clearing away with everybody thinking it would teach her a lesson, when Rick went to wake her up. On opening the bed-room door he found that Murphy had jumped on top of her while she was lying in the bed, pinned her down with the duvet tight around her (she weighed six-and-a-half stone, he weighed fifteen-and-a-half) and was gently huffing dog's breath in her face.

Apparently, every time she had opened her mouth to call for help, he had given her a lovely smacking French kiss which somewhat discouraged her from trying again. She had been pinned there for some seventy minutes because Murphy was very comfortable and would not move. She never came down late for breakfast again!

Terry Moule

Sit – good girl!

When my granddaughter, Samantha, was about two, she loved coming out with me and my dog, Ben, to get the newspaper from our local shop. When we reached the kerb, I gave Ben the command to sit. When he did not respond, I repeated '*Sit*' again very firmly. I turned to see what the tug was on my other hand to find Samantha obediently sitting on the kerb!

Jan King

Eat your hat!

I am President of our local WI, and awhile ago our group organized a Fun Evening and I had to come up with an idea for a hat depicting a town. My idea was ingenious – Chippenham – guessed quite quickly by the members – I can't think why! Blue straw hat (bought for a wedding) with the addition of labels off two well-known brands of ham stuck around the crown, and some micro-waved chips hanging from bits of string around the brim.

Heady with my success, I decided to keep the hat as a topic of conversation for when my grandchildren came to stay. Putting it carefully in the spare room, I firmly shut the door – or so I thought. One day, I went upstairs with my duster and vacuum cleaner and began picking up little bits of . . . ? I wasn't quite sure what for a moment. But then I saw my hat with string hanging and not a single chip in sight. I had thought I had microwaved the chips until they were rock-solid. Penny, our Westie, obviously thought otherwise.

Marian Beale

Eggs away

When we were first married we lived in a caravan in a field belonging to a farmer. One day Rocky, our yellow Labrador, leapt into the caravan wagging his tail – and body – vigorously, with his mouth slightly open and orange-shaped. Placing my hand under his mouth I asked him to 'give' and he promptly put a hen's egg into my hand. I patted his head, told him he was a good boy and gave him a reward. The egg was in perfect condition, no cracks.

This event, since the hens were free range and laid their eggs all over the place, became a daily occurrence. I should add that the hens did not belong to us, so we were really rather naughty to keep them!

One day Rocky did his usual trick, gave me the egg but refused the reward. I then noticed that he had a further egg in his mouth. He had carried both eggs together and neither of them was broken. Needless to say, we had to put an end to this little game or pay the farmer for the eggs.

Mrs Olwyn Allen

Road rage!

We were in the habit of leaving our dog, Monty, in the car outside a shop, and he would start barking as soon as we entered it. Fortunately, we couldn't hear him once we were inside doing what we had to do. We were, however, dismayed, when a lady came in and asked in a loud voice that caused all the other customers to turn and look, 'Does anyone here own the car with the dog in it?' We dutifully owned up, expecting the usual comments that we should not leave the dog in the car, but, instead, she asked us to come outside. All the people in the shop came outside and looked, too.

There was Monty sitting in the driver's seat, obviously tired of barking, and intermittently pressing the horn instead. This, I might add, is now a regular occurrence.

Ellen Levin

SK: Nag! Nag! Hot weather often results in tragedy for pets left in cars. Please remember to leave windows and sun-roof ajar and a bowl of water for your pet.

Art lover

Vicky, our Springer Spaniel, is elderly, overweight and has failing eyesight, but she is an habitual glutton who still retains a keen sense of smell and good hearing – able to detect a cornflake drop on a carpet at a hundred yards.

After Christmas my art student son, for reasons best

known only to him, decided to make a model of a dodo out of the Christmas turkey carcass (which was retrieved from a tree in the garden where it had been hanging for the birds for several weeks). This model, with the aid of wire coat-hangers, newspaper and bits of string was finally completed, photographed and stored in the garage. My son returned to college with the intention of taking it with him on his next visit when he was less overloaded with luggage.

What we failed to realize was that the minute particles of flesh that remained on the carcass were now very 'high' – and were soon detected by the very keen nostrils of Vicky.

On returning from a shopping trip I discovered Vicky looking extremely furtive and rating a good 9.9 on the 'Up-to-no-good' scale. I soon found to my horror that she had located Dodo, devoured the entire carcass, but drawn the line at the wire and bits of string – which was all that remained of my son's precious work of art.

Carol Vinciguerra

Rocky I and II

I: Rocky was a beautiful rough-haired English Collie, but, somehow or other, his brains never seemed to match his personal charm. Either he was thick, or he had a lousy memory. Turn your back, and at the first opportunity Rocky was off – missing – gone – vanished – leaving everyone searching frantically for him. He could never ever remember where he lived, so his usual trick was to tag on to someone and follow them to wherever they were going, relying on them to bring him home, or to contact us or the police with information as to his whereabouts.

This was normal procedure until, one day, when out on one of his escapades, the telephone rang, and a lady's voice at the other end of the line said, 'Mr. Peel? This is the convent. I believe we have your dog. Could you, please, come and collect him?'

From then on, this became a regular occurrence – Rocky had got religion. The Mother Superior, poor soul, must have added our number to the automatic dialling system of her telephone. Eventually, the phone would ring and the voice would say 'It's Sister Agnes. Rocky has had his lunch. Could he come home now?'

II: This behaviour continued until we moved to our present home – a new house on a new estate. As you know, all new estates look the same – lots of houses in various stages of completion, muddy roads and gardens like bomb-sites, each plot of land being marked out with two-by-two posts about two-feet-six stuck in the ground and a length of two-by-two nailed along the top of them. Such was the situation when, about a week or so after moving in, we were awakened in the very early hours of the morning by a great barking commotion. Freda, my wife, thinking that Rocky had been caught short, so to speak, popped her slippers on and went downstairs in her night attire – a pair of pants and one of my T-shirts.

Having let the dog out, Freda then realized that Rocky was not in need of a call of nature, but intent on seeing off an intruder – a cat. Not wanting to awaken the whole neighbourhood by yelling at Rocky, Freda decided that the only thing to do was to set off after him and bring him back. You can imagine the scene, the cat haring up the gardens with Rocky in hot pursuit, followed by Freda, in T-shirt and pants, doing the high hurdles in the rain.

Unfortunately, unknown to Freda, someone, about four plots further up, had made a start on their garden, removing all the builder's rubble and making the best of what topsoil was available. This meant that, at this fence, the take-off side was higher than the landing side. At this point Freda came to grief, going A-over-H into the hole on the other side.

Eventually, Rocky was led home by his pursuer, who was covered in muck and manure, and making all kinds of threats, and generally casting aspersions on the dog's parentage.

Mr Peel

Caught in the act

A few years ago I had a very naughty dog called Sam. On this particular occasion, on arrival home from work, my neighbour called me into the garden.

'Sam', she said, 'has been in my fridge in the garage.'

They had two fridges, and the overflow was in the garage for defrosting, which was why the door was left slightly ajar.

'Oh, what's he done now?' I asked nervously.

'Stolen some ham I was defrosting,' she replied.

'How do you know it was Sam?' I asked defensively.

'Because his paw-print is in the butter!' she said triumphantly.

   Jackie Hall

Taxi!

We once had a large, powerful, friendly yellow Labrador,
called Winston, who just knew that everybody loved him!
One day, after a great day on the beach, we were heading
back to the car-park, with my friend in charge of Winston
on his lead.

   Unfortunately, one of Winston's great joys was riding
in cars. As the day was hot, there was a gentleman seated
in the front passenger-seat of his car, reading his paper,
with the door opened. Seconds later, I heard a surprised
cry. Looking round, I saw that Winston had dived into
the car, and gone straight through the newspaper on to
the driver's seat. The startled cry was from my friend,
who, still clutching the lead, was now lying in the lap of
a gentleman, with a very amazed look on his face.

   Sheila Rapley

I say . . . this *is* fun

We have a lovely Labrador, called Bach, eighteen weeks
old. One day last week he made a mess on the garden
path, so my husband pulled out the garden hose to clear
it up, laid the hose on the path, and went round the corner
to turn the water full on. By the time he came back to
clear up the mess, Bach had picked up the end of the hose
in his mouth and run through the kitchen and the lounge,
watering, watering everywhere.

Trouble is, it's very hard trying to tell a dog off when you are falling about laughing.

Jeannine Terran

99, please

Years ago my Mum and Dad ran a small hotel at Woolacombe, North Devon. We were very busy in the summer months and our beloved Spaniel 'Mr Chips' did not, perhaps, get all the attention he wanted some days. One evening a guest said, 'Your dog looks just like the one down at the Red Barn' (the local ice cream parlour/café). He did – he was the *same* dog! We soon discovered that Mr Chips was turning over his water bowl, a small enamelled pudding basin, and carrying it the mile along the front to the café. He then went from table to table sitting begging for ices which he got!

Lynda Fraser

Waste not, want not

My Grandmother, who was staying with us, was in the kitchen preparing a plaice fillet for her lunch. All of a sudden we heard an anguished cry – Micky, the cat, had run off with the plaice. Tony, the terrier, dashed into the kitchen and chased the cat over several gardens. Five minutes later he returned, head held high, and dropped the very muddy fish at my Grandmother's feet. Being a very Victorian lady of the waste-not-want-not brigade, she washed the plaice and continued to prepare and cook it for her lunch.

Mrs Kathy Smith

Pete the Piddling Pup

A farmer's dog once came to town whose Christian
    name was Pete
His pedigree was ten yards long, his looks were hard
    to beat.
And as he trotted down the street, 'twas beautiful to see
His work on every corner, his work on every tree.

He watered every gateway, he never missed a post,
Piddling was his masterpiece, and piddling was his
    boast.
The city dogs stood looking on with deep and jealous
    rage,
To see this simple country dog the piddler of his age.

They smelt him over one by one, they smelt him two
    by two,

The noble Pete, in big disdain stood still to labour
through.
They sniffed him over one by one, their praise for
him ran high,
But when one sniffed him underneath Pete piddled
in his eye.

Then just to show those city dogs he didn't care a
damn,
He strolled into a grocer's shop and piddled on his
ham.
He piddled on his onions, he piddled on his floor,
And when the grocer kicked him out he piddled on
his door.

They showed him all the piddling posts they knew
about the town,
They started off with many winks to wear the stranger
down.
But Pete was with them every trick with vigour and
with vim,
A thousand piddles more or less were all the same to
him.

So on and on went noble Pete with hind legs kicking
high,
While most were lifting legs in bluff and piddling
mighty dry.
And on and on went noble Pete and watered every
sandhill,

'Til one and all the city dogs were piddled to a
    standstill.

Then Pete an exhibition gave in all the ways to piddle,
Like double drips and fancy flips and now and then
    a dribble.
And all this time the country dog did neither wink
    nor grin,
But blithely piddled out of town the way he piddled
    in.

The city dogs said 'So long Pete your piddling did
    defeat us',
But no-one ever put them wise that Pete had diabetes!
    Sent in by Joan and Paul Cardus: author unknown

A very peculiar practice

Some years ago – in the days when we were allowed a
sense of humour – I was a policeman in Kent. One of
my colleagues was more or less permanently on duty at
the enquiry (front) office where the public comes in to
tell you anything and everything. One day a lady entered
with a small mongrel dog she had found. Having done
the basic paperwork – name and address of finder, day,
date, time, etc., etc., my colleague breathed a sigh of
relief as he reached the final section: 'Has the dog any
distinguishing marks, features, peculiarities, madam?' he
enquired.

The lady, everybody's mum-type, replied, almost
proudly: 'He's *very* intelligent.'

My colleague put his pen down, leant over the counter and looked down at the lost dog, which returned his gaze.

'Right *you*,' he said, 'what's your name and address?'

The lady, obviously convinced she was saving the dog from the hands of a mad man wearing a police uniform, started to back off, saying: '*Please* don't worry. *I'll* find his owner.'

Bob Ansell

Chihuahua-Cross from hell!

Charlie, our Chihuahua, is better known as 'the schizophrenic'. We have had him from a five-week-old pup, and he is now four. He is treated like a spoilt child, and we never know what he will do next.

Charlie sleeps on the bed between my wife and me. (He has a large beanbag and a lovely warm basket, but they are not good enough for him.) When it gets cold, he steals the duvet *somehow*, rolls over and over, wraps it round himself and we wake up blue with cold. When we get ready for bed and say we are going upstairs, Charlie is always first up and in the bed. He immediately lies with his head on my pillow and I have to fight him for my place. If I get up to go to the loo, the battle starts all over again – and he has bitten me over this! I get up for work around 2 a.m. As soon as I sit on the edge of the bed waking up, he moves into my place (head on pillow). He will not get up in the morning until the fire is lit and the room is warm.

Charlie will only eat his meat if my wife feeds him with a fork. He will not eat sweets or chocolate, but will eat radishes, raw cabbage, and carrots are his favourite. If you try to read the paper and he does not want you to, he sits on the paper to ensure you can't. He also believes he is a fox fur, and will lie on his back wrapped round your neck with his tongue in your earhole. Recently, we took him to the local shops and, as I waited outside with Charlie window-shopping, my foot felt suddenly warm: Charlie had cocked his leg up and watered me. If he is in the chair, or on the settee, you have to give way because he won't. He attacks any size dog as long as he is in the house and the other dog is outside!

We went to see our son in Plymouth. He has a very large Bull Staff, and when this dog came down the path, Charlie ran up my back and on to my shoulders. No-one can say how he did this because it happened so fast no-one saw him do it. When my wife washes her hair she has to dry Charlie's, too, or he sulks.

I swear this is all true. I have always had big dogs before and Charlie is definitely a one-off! He comes to you for fussing, but when you start to fuss him, he immediately has a go at you.

Alan Davie

Football hooligan

Our present companion is Harvey, a superb Golden Retriever who is football crazy – not like other dogs simply pushing a ball around with their noses, but actually dribbling the ball with his feet, pulling the football back with his front paws and kicking it expertly forwards with his rear ones.

This created a great deal of amusement for the local youngsters, until such time when Harvey's ball skills developed to the point where the lads were unable to retrieve the ball back from him. Then, as Harvey approached, the cry would go out, 'Look out, here comes Gazza – pick the ball up'.

One day, after a great deal of time spent begging and paw-offering to the boy clutching the ball, Harvey, realizing the futility of the exercise, transferred his attention to the 'goal posts'. A good sniff around, a quick turn, and suddenly a rear leg was raised purposefully high in the air. Immediately, there was a scramble of young footballers rushing downfield to recover their jackets and jumpers from the ground around the goalpost. Harvey, meanwhile, of course, took his chance and dribbled the ball down the field to score at the other end.

Harvey is now suspended. A case of ungentlemanly conduct and he's on the transfer list.

Mr Peel

Welcome HAM!

I can't remember much about the war as I was born in June 1940, but I can clearly remember the day my uncle (Godfather) arrived home after six years away in the Army. Everyone was very excited about his arrival and my Gran had queued for hours to get the luxury of some boiled ham. With everything still on ration, she had only managed to get a small amount, and, to make it look more on the plates, she had opened some corned beef. The table was set as posh as possible for the great homecoming, with a mixture of ham and corned beef placed neatly on each plate.

Our dog, at that time, was called Monty. My Gran was rather afraid of dogs, so poor Monty was never allowed to visit her, but, on this very special day, I insisted that Uncle Leo would want to see him and Gran reluctantly agreed that he could come along for the celebrations.

Suddenly, on the Big Day, there was a knock at the door, and we all went out to meet our hero. Having closed the living-room door to keep him from running out, no-one bothered about Monty.

Eventually, after the greetings had been exchanged, we went into the living-room for tea. Monty looked a little bit 'sheepish'. All the ham had disappeared off each plate. Monty preferred ham to corned beef.

My Gran lived until the age of eighty, so several dogs came and went in our lives after Monty, but no dog was ever again allowed to visit her.

Ruth Shaw

Is there a lobster in the house?

We had invited ten good friends for a lobster supper. In the morning my husband collected twelve lobsters which I arranged beautifully on beds of mustard-and-cress on two basket trays. With the salad pre-prepared, all I had to do was to cook a few potatoes when our guests arrived. After a few pre-supper drinks I took off to the kitchen and was aghast to be greeted by bits of mustard-and-cress all over the floor. Heart beating faster than ever before, I then took in that only two of the lobsters were left on the tray and that five yellow Labradors were now sleeping soundly. They had eaten the other ten lobsters, including shells, whiskers – everything but the mustard-and-cress.

'Don't panic,' my husband, John, said, when I coaxed him into the kitchen and panic-strickenly told him the score. 'Keep them all drinking while I drive back to the lobster restaurant and buy ten more.'

One hour later, he returned triumphantly and, at the strawberries-and-cream stage, we entertained our completely 'blotto' guests with the lobster-happy Labradors' story.

It was the most expensive supper party we ever gave – and doubtless the best meal the dogs ever had!

Nancy Dove

Great escape

Gin, our Cairn Terrier, was a notorious Houdini and caused us much anxiety because we lived close to a busy main road. He adored children, and when ours were at school he sought consolation in other schools in the area (all of which were on the other side of the main road). Teachers would phone to say that Gin was in the play-ground or classroom, and when he ventured as far as the Grammar School, my embarrassed son would be summoned to bring him home on the end of his school tie!

Having repaired and re-netted the perimeter of our large garden to no avail, my husband decided that we must replace the fencing. Soon after these new expensive palings were (professionally) installed, I was in my bed-room and heard a strange noise. I looked out – and lo and behold – Gin was tearing at, chewing and spitting out small splinters of wood from the new fence. Judging by the size of the hole he had already made, he was intent on making it big enough for the other dogs (one a large Golden Retriever) to follow him through! They were just sitting quietly behind him, waiting patiently!

We never won the Great Escape Battle with Gin, but he lived to be nearly nineteen-and-a-half, and all that he suffered from in old age was the loss of most of his teeth!

Audrée Abbott

A very happy Christmas

Our lovely old Red Setter, Rufus, has various allergies and his staple diet is turkey or fish, rice and potato. Three or four years ago, I made four Christmas cakes. They were not quite cold at bedtime, so I covered them as best I could and left them on the dining-table safe from our two thieving cats.

The next morning my daughter, Angela, and I were up early as we planned to go Christmas shopping. Angela took Rufus out for his early walk and returned very agitated because he had been in the river most of the time drinking gallons of water and did not want his breakfast. Very worrying – so instead of catching the 9 a.m. train we went to the vet. The vet was quite concerned, too. Rufus had a very tender tummy and was very dehydrated.

Eventually, with heavy hearts, we set off to do our shopping, leaving Rufus in the tender care of my husband who assured us he would immediately ring the vet if Rufus got any worse. Needless to say we cut our trip short and, on our return, found Rufus no better but no worse.

Some time later Angela went into the dining-room and said, 'That's funny. What is this crunched-up foil doing on the floor?' We then discovered that Rufus had eaten a whole Christmas cake! As it had some of my husband's best brandy in it, no wonder he was dehydrated!

Jennifer R. Beetham

My Jane

She doesn't bring me my paper,
She seldom sits up and begs,
She never carries my slippers,
And is forever banging my legs.
Her nose mists up my windows,
And she chews up half my shoes,
She claws ladders in my stockings,
'Till I have to wear my trews.

She won't walk to heel –
To her that's just a joke.
She puffs and pulls at her collar,
'Till I'm sure she's going to choke.

She chases cats and rolls around
In puddles and in mud.
Then won't shake off a single drop,
'Till we get home and face the flood.

She barks when excited,
And jumps all over my friends.
If I put her in the living-room
She just scratches till their visit ends.
And who wants a dog like that?

But when the whole world's against me,
And nobody really cares.
When I give up the struggle,

And sink down on the stairs –
Up comes my beauty
To nuzzle in my thigh
And, with paws up on my shoulders and chest,
She kisses me in the eye.

And when I crawl home late
With an aching head,
Feeling so tired and so weary
And ready just for bed –
I know that she'll greet me
In leaps and several bounds,
So how could I change her
Even for one-million pounds?

She's my Jane.
(An Alsatian.)

Denise Leighton

SK: Denise, I think your sentiments truly sum up the spirit of this book.

Love me . . . love my dog

Enclosed is a photostat copy of the instructions given to my friend, Nellie, when she agreed to look after Dinky Doodle Bugs, her granddaughter's dog. Nellie is a very young octogenarian, not a bit dithery or the least senile, 'though even Nellie's best friend would agree she does sometimes have trouble adjusting her hearing aid. Still, since Nellie had her pace-maker fitted, nobody can keep up with her to hear what she is saying!

Dinky Doodle Bugs duly arrived at Nellie's, complete with his meat, biscuits, toys *and* the following lists of instructions.

1. Feed her when you like a.m., but keep it to that time.
2. Don't mash her food up, just take out of tin and sprinkle biscuits on her meat and by it.
3. *Fresh Water*. Change it twice a day at least.
4. If hot weather she won't eat until evening but just leave the dish down and she will eat it when she wants it. If she seems ill, *Get Mum Now. Don't Wait*.
5. If she doesn't eat it, change it. Open another tin next day. If she doesn't eat that, *Get Mum*. Does she seem ill? If so, *Get Mum Now*.
6. Don't feed her meat that's been about for a few days. *She Will Shit Everywhere*.
7. Give her freshly cooked and well-cooked food only.
8. She can eat cake, sweets and choc, but not too big bits as she ain't got many teeth left.
9. *Don't Feed Her Bones Ever*.
10. Keep all poisons and pellets *Away* from her.
11. She will sleep in the chair during the day, basket at night in your bedroom.
12. She understands, '*Up The Garden*', '*Going To Bed*', '*In Your Basket*'.
13. *Don't Pick Her Up – You'll Hurt Her*.
14. She will ask to go up the garden. She will start moaning and running about. *You* won't hear her whine

and moan, so keep an eye out. She wees a lot less times than you do, so don't worry. She can be left about eight-to-twelve hours. But you must make her go up the garden before you go out then she will be okay. You say '*Up The Garden*' and off she'll go.

15. Any problems: Contact *Mum*. *If In Doubt, Ask Mum Immediately. Don't Wait.*

16. Let her have a few minutes on her own up the garden, but keep an eye out for her as she may try to go next door.

17. If she's ill, *Get Mum. Don't Dither. Get Mother.* Get Mum to take her to the vet straight away. Don't have her put down unless she's *really really really really really* ill and suffering.

    The last time they said 'put her down' she went to animal hospital instead and that was six years ago, so they don't know it all. *I DON'T CARE ABOUT THE MONEY I JUST LOVE MY DOG WITH ALL MY HEART.*

18. She does not need walks. So don't worry.

19. She will wander around you all the time, so don't stand on her. She will roam around the garden with you, but *Don't Forget* she's with you. *Don't Lock* her in the shed.

Thank you for looking after her. See you soon. Love Nic.
    John Langridge

Another nuisance call!

When Benjie, my Labrador pup, was about three months old, I was talking to a friend on my hall phone when, suddenly, there seemed to be someone else on the line. We thought it was a crossed line. However, when I put the phone down and went into the sitting-room, Benjie had the phone off the hook and was very excited, presumably because he had recognized my voice. For a few days afterwards he kept lifting the phone and stood listening to the recording of the lady telling him to replace the handset.

He is now six months and still full of mischief.

Mrs Betty Hamilton

Feeling sheepish

It was a crisp sunny winter's day and my daughter and I set out to walk our three Golden Retrievers – Bonnie, Pickle and Pepper – on a nearby beach. It was a bit of a treat for them and excitement was at fever pitch. As I opened the hatchback, out they all bounded, up and over the dunes, heading for the beach.

My daughter and I followed at a more leisurely pace, expecting to find all three dogs waiting for us on the beach. Sure enough, Bonnie and Pepper ran up to us, but Pickle was nowhere to be seen. We called and called but there was no sign of her. Thinking she may have returned to the car we retraced our steps over the dunes and looked towards the car-park. There we beheld an absolutely incredible scenario.

Near a parked car, in a circle, sat a white Poodle, a

white Westie, two yellow Labradors, a strange Retriever and our Pickle. All were completely under the spell of an old Border Collie. The Collie's owner apologized profusely, explaining that her dog imagined all pale-coloured dogs were sheep and insisted on rounding them up and herding them!

Hilary Searle

Anyone for bed?

This is the tale of Jumbo and poor old Grannie Johnston who ended her days bedridden, and a permanent occupant of bedroom Number Three. Jumbo was a very large Labrador-cum-whatever, a huge old Silly-Billy who had a coat that was black as night and as thick as a fireside rug. He moulted twice a year and, much to everybody's annoyance, always left large tufts of fur carelessly strewn here and there. These had to be hand-picked up, otherwise they put the old-fashioned vacuum cleaner out of commission.

Grannie Johnston's mattress was supported by a wire-spring frame, and, pre-bedtime (his) Jumbo would go under the bed and, with his back hunched, go round and round in circles, as dogs do. Each time he passed under Grannie Johnston's body, she would, much to her enjoyment, be lifted and bumped upwards. We always knew when Jumbo was doing his pre-bedtime circles because we would hear Grannie Johnston's squeaks of satisfaction.

During Jumbo's moulting time, it was an almost daily chore for yours-truly to get under the bed and remove all the tufts of fur trapped in the springs. On one occasion I found, in addition to Jumbo's fur, pieces of the skin of a breakfast sausage that had gone missing from the larder some days previously. Jumbo had remained quiet while Dad was being accused of never having brought the sausage home in the first place.

   Roy Coleman

All shook up!

Separating our garden from that of our neighbours' is a long line of what we thought were impenetrable nine-feet-high conifers. Usually Monty, our rescued German Shepherd, snuffles along the base of the conifers, peering through tiny gaps to eye up the cats sunning themselves on the neighbours' lawn just a few feet beyond.

Then came the fateful night. It was about ten p.m., and

we were lazily watching TV, wondering whether to call it a night, when there was a knock on the door. It was the lady from two doors down. 'Have you got an Alsatian?' she asked. 'Yes,' we replied. 'Oh,' she said, matter-of-factly, 'it's in our swimming-pool.'

We later deduced that the following had happened.

Monty, having finally cracked under the strain of not being able to get at the cats, had launched himself Red Rum fashion through our domestic version of Becher's Brook, landing on next door's soft and hitherto immaculate lawn. The cats naturally fled towards the next garden, scrambling up, over, and down the other side of the wall. Monty, naturally expecting another lawn to appear on the other side of the wall, had leapt with all the grace and majesty of a gazelle, realized his mistake in full flight, and belly-flopped into the swimming-pool. The panic which had galvanized the cats into such unseemly haste, had, alas, a similar effect on the neighbours who were, until that moment, enjoying a quiet summer evening pool-side barbecue.

We arrived at the scene to find water everywhere, and the head and front paws of Monty clinging on for dear life to the side of the pool. Monty stared at us, tongue out, over-large ears accentuated by the wet fur and security spot lights. 'What have you done!', the ears dropped. 'Get out.' 'He can't,' said our neighbour in that same matter-of-fact voice, 'he's stuck.'

Eventually, after much huffing-and-puffing, we managed to get Monty on to dry land (but only after the neighbour had got into the pool and pushed from behind).

Once out, Monty gave himself a good wholesome shake covering everyone with yet more water. Then, because there is no side entrance to our neighbours' house, and access to and from the garden is through the house itself, I had to steer Monty by his scruff (in our panic we had forgotten the lead). As we reached the lounge, Monty decided to have another shake, then another in the kitchen, in the hall, and over the car parked on the driveway. Making my apologies, I made off with my dog – my body at a low crouch with his mane firmly in grip.

Miraculously, our neighbours still speak to us, and I have now imposed a strict curfew on night-time patrols. As for Monty, he seems to have settled down a little . . . apart, that is, from the time he chewed my unopened wage packet . . .

William Hatcher

My faithful friend – dedicated to Mitsi

A faithful dog will play with you,
Will laugh with you, will cry.
He'll gladly starve to stay with you,
and never reason why.

And when you're feeling out of sorts,
Somehow he'll understand.
Will watch you with his shining eyes
and try to lick your hand.

And when everything is said and done,
It really isn't odd,
For when you spell Dog backwards
you get the name of GOD!

Trish Jones

To Amber with love

Our yellow Labrador, Amber, has now reached three years
old, hence the following poem.

You've brought us joy beyond compare
(and quite a bit of golden hair).
You're always happy, never cross
(as long as you can be the boss).

And now you've grown up to be three
We're all adults here (you, Sue and me).
And we'll all behave in an adult way
(we'll throw the ball, so you can play).

Here's to another year of cuddles
(we'll tidy up – you make the muddles).
But no-one can match the love we send,
to a little *bitch*, but a perfect friend.

Sue and Ron Hurrell

Jog on, old chap!

My brother's dogs are both Collie-cross-Labs. Bernard
is large, square, black-and-white, and Pepper is black.
They spend a lot of time at the school next door, love

the children and especially love going jogging with them.

Well, one day a few weeks ago – life was pretty boring – the children were on holiday, and the dogs were really fed up. Until, lo and behold, they heard the pitter-patter of joggers outside the gate! Off the two bounded, only to find that it was not the children, but two chaps from the nearby Air Base. Never mind, when you are into serious training like Berny and Pep, well what the heck . . . Anyway, there was not anything else to do! Berny and Pep 'fell in' behind the chaps and off they all went. We are not really sure whether the two men noticed them or not.

On they jogged, passing the end of the little track which marked the end of their usual jogging route with the children! Berny, of course, did mention this to Pep, but on and on they jogged. 'Phew' getting a bit tired now and a little worried. Eventually they reached the main road (seriously worried now) and jogged on until they reached the gates to the Air Base manned by police etc.

Now extremely anxious and a long way from home, Berny realized that the two men had passes and, of course, as he pointed out to Pep, they did not! He then suggested that they beat a hasty retreat back across the road, through some other gates and make a Flight-of-the-Bumble-Bee line home along the runway!

All Air Base flights were then stopped for about an hour while someone in authority endeavoured to apprehend them. Pep was caught quite quickly, but Bernard was a little more tricky. Then someone, who happens to know my brother, came back on duty, contacted the man on the runway and asked him to describe the dogs.

'Try calling him Bernard,' he said.

'Got him,' was the triumphant reply.

Bridget Clark

Anyone for . . . dogs and ladders?

As a young man, my father had a devoted black Labrador called Monty and, when he was on leave from doing his National Service, Monty, having been deprived of his beloved master's company for several months, spent the whole day glued to my father's side. At the time, my grandmother was also looking after several of her nieces and nephews who were delighted to see their older cousin and pestered him at regular intervals throughout the days.

A problem with roof-tiles required my father's presence on the roof. He duly set up the ladder, climbed to the top and started work. At various times when he was standing on the top rungs of the ladder, the ladder was shaken from below. Eventually he called over his shoulder to his mother, insisting that she stop the children playing at the foot of the ladder. No response, so he kept shouting. Then he turned to look down – no children, no mother – but, right behind him, on the ladder, tail vigorously wagging, was Monty, delighted that he had, at long last, managed to reach his master.

The climb up had apparently been simple – but getting Monty down was another matter. The only way this could be safely accomplished was by my father climbing on to the roof and coaxing Monty up and off the ladder to join

him. For some reason, Monty was not exactly enthusiastic about this. Once there, however, my father could pick him up and carry him back down the ladder – not a simple feat since Monty was no small animal. Both lived to tell the tale!

    Janice Griffiths

Hi there! Wait for me . . .

In 1991 we took on an Irish Red Setter from the Bristol rescue people. Sophie was about three years old – in an awful state physically, having been starved to about half her normal weight and locked in a flat all day. But mentally she appeared okay – okay, that is, for an Irish Red Setter, and she had a really wonderful temperament. Within a few months she was transformed – her weight was about correct, her coat magnificent, and she could run like a race horse.

One lovely summer's day, she was running free on the Common when she spied a canine chum about three-hundred yards away across the valley. Off she shot . . .

However, between her and her chum was one contented owner. He and his lady wife were stretched out on the grassy slope, lying head to feet along Sophie's flight path, having a peaceful snooze.

To compound the calamity, Sophie, now at full pelt, had to skid to a halt beside her new buddy. So, not content with running over the full length of this poor man's body, she also used him as a panic-braking area.

He was not amused and we were mortified. To this

day I don't know how he (eventually) took it so well –
particularly when Sophie finished the episode with huge,
wet, sloppy licks.

Andy Barr

Just trying to be helpful

About forty years ago, my father, Alf Snow, had a black
Retriever called Steve. One day, while still a young dog,
Steve went off for a walk-about. My parents were very
upset and reported his loss to the police. Luckily, within
twenty-four hours, the police contacted them to say that
a dog answering the description had been brought in.
Would they come and see if it was theirs.

Off Dad trotted and was happy to see Steve; and Steve,
of course, was happy to see Dad. The constable on the desk
was completing the usual paperwork and the conversation
went thus:

P.C.: 'How old is your dog, Sir?'

Dad: 'About eight months, I think.'

P.C.: 'Do you know for sure, Sir? I think this dog
looks about five months old to me, Sir.'

Dad: 'No, I'm pretty sure it's about eight months.'
(Dad was *never* wrong about anything.)

P.C.: 'Well, Sir, you do surprise me. If I was asked, I
would definitely say this dog was not a day over
six months!'

Dad: 'No, I remember now when we got it. The dog
is definitely eight months old.' (He knew he was
winning now.)

P.C: 'Well, Sir, if you are absolutely certain the dog

is eight months old, then I shall have to fine you for not having a dog licence!'
Lindsay Wade

You must be joking!

I have two Pekinese and one, Chan, has recently been troubled with a possible kidney infection or even stones. In order to help with the diagnosis I was asked, if possible, to get a water sample. So, armed with the sample bottle Chan and I went around the garden on innumerable occasions but with no luck. He always chose the lawn, gravel drive or garden borders – never a flat surface where I could put down a suitable receptacle to collect the sample.

By now, we were due back at the vet's and I had nothing to take. Then I hit on the idea that when we went to the vet's, Chan would get out of the car and would immediately cock his leg up in the car park. So, off we went for our appointment armed with the sample bottle. Once out of the car, Chan immediately looked for the 'right' spot to perform. *No luck* – he did not fancy here or there. But, as we went through the car-park, *bingo*, up went his leg and, yes, down the only drain in the car-park went the only possible sample!

A small – *very* small – sample was obtained later and we are now being treated for stones.
Miss Julia Briars

Happy birthday, everyone

My friend Jo has a Weimaraner bitch named Gretel who is a walking dustbin.

About four years ago, when Jo's elder son was about

five, she planned a birthday treat for him. He and a few friends were taken to a pantomime matinée, and everyone was taken back afterwards for a birthday tea, which was set out on the table, before leaving, with sufficient goodness to feed several children and accompanying adults.

On arrival home, Jo triumphantly threw open the dining-room door saying 'Do come and have tea'. The table was *empty*, and a very bloated and ill-looking Gretel was lying on the floor. (She had, of course, been shut out of the dining-room, but had managed to open the high-latch cottage-style door during everybody's absence!)

I am not quite sure what the party had for tea – not much I suspect – but Gretel didn't eat for two days afterwards.

Mrs Jill Jackson

So what!

When my nephew was two or three my brother took him to see the Royal Tournament. As usual the dog display team did its act and the audience was hushed while one dog carefully balanced his way along two narrow beams. When he safely reached the other side everyone cheered and applauded – except my nephew!

'Don't you think he's a clever dog to do that?' asked his Dad.

'No,' came the reply, 'that's nothing. If they'd got a cat it could have walked along *one* beam, and it could have done it without being trained!'

Ruth Kime

First things first

When our family dog died I had the sad task of telling my son when he came in from school that his pet had been run over. I told him very gently, softening the blow with stories of doggy heaven and celestial walkies etc., all the while waiting for the floods of tears. I need not have worried . . . when the whole sorry saga was finished, his first question was 'What sort of car was it?'

Angela Matthews

Seeing stars!

While on a camping holiday I slept on a camp-bed in the lounge area of the tent as the bedroom area was full of the rest of the family. One night, while lying on my camp-bed, with our two dogs tied to my ankles to ensure

they did not stray, a noise was heard outside. Gemma the faithful guard dog and Fred Boxer the dim-witted back-up awoke and listened to decide if action was needed. The next few seconds went so fast I am not sure what happened but, from lying asleep on the bed, I next found myself outside the tent, looking up at the night sky, the dogs still attached to my ankles.

Thankfully no-one had been about to see me being yanked under the tent door and dragged unceremoniously out into the field, so I quickly tried to nip back in, but saw more stars as I hit the un-zipped door. Ouch!

Miss S. M. Horniblow

Getting his come-uppance

Years ago, my daughter Katie's bedroom overlooked the garden and our newly acquired West Highland White Terrier used to wait until she came into the kitchen for breakfast then race into her room, leap in the air, land on her bed, and remain, forepaws on the windowsill, back legs on the bed, monitoring all that went on in the garden.

Furthermore, on washdays, he liked to grab knickers or whatever from the pile of dirty washing and race down the hallway. He would then stop just outside my daughter's bedroom and stand glaring defiance at my wife. As soon as she made a move to retrieve the garment, he would disappear at speed under the bed and defy all attempts to lure him out.

One day he got his come-uppance.

Having decided we needed more storage space, we bought my daughter a new bed with divan drawers. Before I went to work that morning I removed the old bed, standing it in the hall downstairs to enable the new bed to be installed. Imagine, if you will, everyone eating breakfast when W.H.W.T. runs into daughter's bedroom in his usual manner, leaps into the air, *No Bed To Land On*, loud crash and accompanying yelp as he hits the floor below the window!

Later that morning, new bed delivered – complete with divan drawers – wife commences to wash removed bedding. W.H.W.T. grabs pillow-case, runs to the doorway of daughter's bedroom, glares defiance in time-honoured fashion, my wife advances on recovery mission, W.H.W.T. tries to dive under the bed at usual thirty

knots, and bashes his head on newly installed divan
drawer.

You will not find these methods in any dog-training
manual, but he never again climbed on a bed or stole
washing.

    Harry Calthorpe

I'm a star!

Some years ago our dramatic society staged Ben Travers'
farce, *Cuckoo in the Nest*, and I was the producer/director.
The cast list calls for a little dog, so our set designer offered
the services of her Jamie; I'm no expert on breeds but I
think he was a Yorkshire Terrier. All went well and, after
a while, we learned that on rehearsal evenings Jamie would
stand by the door at home, waiting to be brought to the
theatre. What we had not considered, however, was the
effect that an audience would have on him. On the Mon-
day evening we staged a performance for Senior Citizens.
As soon as Jamie made his entrance he caught sight of the
ladies in the front row (we think one or two might have
spoken to him), walked over to the front of the stage and
barked and barked.

The next evening I decided that he should be tied by
his lead to a kitchen chair to keep him away from the
front of the stage. Well, how was I to know that even he
would be more than a match for a chair with *no-one sitting
on it*? Once again he caught sight of the audience and
walked over to bark at them – towing the chair behind
him.

On the Wednesday evening we tied him to a heavy

kitchen table. That kept him in his place all right, but he remained the star of the show and we heard that some people were buying tickets to come again just to see what he would do next.

Norman Bodicoat

Glue sniffer!

Our late Springer Spaniel, Tina Popelowski (her kennel name), had an insatiable appetite. My wife, a teacher, in preparation for making papier mâché models with her class, had combined more than half a bucket of flour and water in a paste to be used as glue. Unsuspectingly, she left the bucket under the sink in the kitchen where Tina Popelowski slept overnight. Well, I need hardly recount our astonishment, when, on groping our way downstairs the following morning, we found one very empty bucket and one very full dog!

Oooh! Arrgh! The very thought of it brings visions of syrup-of-figs and other laxatives immediately to mind. For at least four days we became the owners of one very round dog who wore an expression of pain and puzzlement, but also triumph at having succeeded in nicking yet one more tasty morsel from under our noses. One might have thought that this would have taught her a lesson, but, oh no, this was just one of many such incidents in her very eventful life.

Jeremy M. D. Moger

Eat your hat!

In the late 1930s, when I was a schoolboy, my parents owned a young and lively Scottie. One day, an electrician came to the house to do some work. He carried a bag of tools, and, in the way of those more formal times, wore a bowler hat. When he had finished his work, he said to my mother:

'Have you seen my hat, Mrs Smith?'

'No,' she replied, 'where did you leave it?'

'I put it on this chair by the kitchen table, but it's not there now.'

So a hunt began for the missing hat, but there was no sign of it. Then mother had an idea.

'It might have fallen off the chair.' She peered under the table.

There, as usual, was the Scottie in his basket, and with him the missing bowler.

'It's here!' she cried.

But, oh dear, it was minus the brim! Father had to buy the man a new hat.

A year later, we had to call on the same electrician's services again. When he was finished, he made ready to go.

'Have you seen my hat, Mrs Smith?'

Heart in mouth, and disbelieving, mother looked under the table into the eye of a contented Scottie. There was the hat, and, thank goodness, the brim was intact. Only the crown was missing!

Alan Smith

Reflections

Treasure each moment, don't be cross
When you find one glove and the other's lost.
When the face gazing up at you seems to say,
'Now *where* did I put that yesterday?'

Don't be cross when the day is done
And he wants to play and have some fun.
When he finds a ball and, as a treat,
Lays it before your aching feet.

Don't be cross when it's pouring with rain
And he wants to go out in the garden again,
When the muddy paws leave an endless track
From the front hall door to the kitchen mat.

Don't be cross when your favourite shrub
Spends most of the time outside of its tub,
When the lawn resembles a putting green,
Full of more holes than you've ever seen.

Treasure each moment, make them last,
For the time will come when they're over and past.
When the soft brown eyes are laid to rest,
Remember he tried to do his best.

Treasure each moment deep in your heart,
For when the time comes and you have to part,

You will know for certain that, come what may,
You wouldn't have changed a single day.

Be grateful and happy for all that you shared,
Content that he knew you really cared.
Treasure each moment and all that's gone,
Then repeat it again with another one.

Shirley A. Symes

One for the birds

Benji, our Jack Russell (long legs and shaggy coat) spends many hours sitting looking down the garden watching the birds. We encourage the birds in and provide water and food regularly. When Benji was younger he jealously chased them away, but now, at thirteen years old and a diabetic, he tolerates them. Well, we thought he did, until we saw him walk over to the birds' drinking water, lift his leg and, with perfect aim, top up the contents.

Patricia van Os

Sorry, Mum . . .

We have a black-and-white Lurcher bitch, named Susie, that we took in from a rescue centre last year. We had not had her very long when, one morning, I was horrified to discover that she had stolen a full packet of paracetamol tablets that I had left on the kitchen worktop. Panic-stricken, I called my husband downstairs. Six-thirty in the morning, the middle of winter, freezing cold and very dark, we searched high and low for the packet, including hunting round the garden, in our dressing gowns, with a torch. Nothing, just a few pieces of chewed cardboard from the outer wrapper.

Thoroughly concerned by now, my husband phoned the vet at his home. He told us to bring Susie straight round to the surgery where he would meet us. We arrived just as he was getting out of his car still struggling to get dressed.

After giving her a quick look over he told us that, if she had swallowed the whole packet it was extremely serious and that her stomach would have to be pumped out immediately. Even then there was no guarantee that her system would not be permanently damaged. He also got on the phone straight away and ordered some special tablets for her.

Really upset we left her in his capable hands and he told us to ring about teatime that same day. Duly ringing at five p.m., we were told that her stomach had been pumped and we could come and collect her. When we arrived he said that, although she was okay at the moment it would be a couple of weeks before we could be sure that no lasting damage had been done, and that she would have to be given the special tablets that had now arrived.

We paid the bill – *fifty-five pounds* – and took her home.

Around seven p.m., that evening I let her out into the garden, and after ten minutes or so decided to go and check on her. I was greeted by her arriving at the back door carrying (you've guessed it) the missing packet of paracetamol, slightly chewed around the edges but all tablets intact.

We were so elated that she had not swallowed the tablets that we forgot about the fifty-five pounds that we had handed to the vet.

Mrs Christine Clark

Don't mess with me!

Emma, our late Yorkshire Terrier, was a small dog weighing less than five pounds, and most of that was heart. Emma was always very protective of us. She had a ferocious deep bark more akin to an Alsatian or Labrador and was totally fearless in her encounters with other canines.

One winter's evening I was walking Emma on the estate where we lived and, as we approached the entrance to an alleyway, she started to growl quietly. Then, as a pair of feet emerged from the dark opening, Emma launched into a spirited volley of barking. The occupant of the emerging boots leapt several feet into the air and, as he came down to earth in the middle of the pavement, now visible in the street-light, I identified him as our six foot, seven-inch community policeman. He was as close to respiratory failure as it is possible to get. Fortunately he saw the funny side and the three of us parted on good terms.

We lived, at this time, in an open-plan house where the stairs ran up from the living-room. Our television went wrong and the engineer came one lunchtime. By this time we also had a psychopathic standard Poodle, called Tara, who accompanied me to the door when the engineer knocked. As I opened the door, one hand restraining Tara, whose favourite pastime was standing on her hind legs, paws outreached towards her victim's shoulders, ready to lick them to death, the engineer stepped back pleading with me to shut Tara in because he was terrified of dogs. I duly shut Tara in the kitchen and the engineer proceeded to tackle the television. He had switched the set on and was manipulating a knitting needle (!) through the rear of the casing, when Emma, who had been asleep upstairs, awoke and detected a stranger on her territory. Launching herself down the stair-case, emitting a terrifying growl, she leapt at the terrified engineer's ankle. There was a blue flash, the television went up in smoke and the engineer needed treatment for shock (Emma-shock!) before taking the television away for extensive repair.

Another of Emma's pet hates were insurance men. Her first victim made the mistake of ignoring her bared gums and growls and proffered his hand to her saying 'You wouldn't bite me, would you?' She sank her razor-sharp teeth into his digit.

Nigel and Ann Franklin

60

Quick thinking!

When he was a toddler my son, Nicholas, had an uncanny knack of putting his foot in it and causing great embarrassment. My parents-in-law telephoned to say that they would be visiting and bringing some Canadian cousins. I dutifully set about laying on a traditional English teatime spread.

On the day of their arrival everything went wrong, but I had managed to clean the dining-room and set the table with the best cutlery and crockery and it looked most attractive. The last cake I had finished was a Victoria sponge, which I had baked and filled and left on the kitchen worktop. I was just about to ice it, when the phone rang and I left the kitchen to answer it. To my horror (and this is where Roxy, the Labrador comes in) when I returned after my epic gossip on the telephone, Roxy had put his paws up on the worktop and helped himself to a bite of sponge cake.

Now, by this time, I neither had the time, nor the eggs, to bake another cake. You might ask yourself, why not just throw it away and manage with explanations and what was on the table? I cannot answer that question sanely, as all I know is that when you are a young mother with two small children and two dogs, you are out to impress and the obvious answer does not always spring to mind. So, I cut out the section with dog teeth-marks which left me with a fat crescent shape. This I masked with a lemon-flavoured butter cream and toasted coconut. I thought it looked very professional.

Everyone arrived and we went to the dining-room,

took our places and tucked into a delicious tea. When it came to the cakes, our Canadian cousins complimented me on my decorated sponge cake, whereupon Nicholas suddenly piped up: 'It wasn't like that to begin with. Roxy took a bite out of it, and Mummy cut it up and decorated it . . . and shouted at Roxy and made him sit in his basket.'

Margaret Lethbridge

Room freshener!

My husband, David, is a keen gardener and, taking pride in our herbaceous borders, he had buried, under a beautiful hosta, a slug-trap filled with beer. After a few days, this mixture was very thick and slimy, and smelt like nothing on earth. Bracken, our Welsh Springer Spaniel, was fascinated by this delectable delight and determined to investigate it. I had already warned him off a couple of times, when, one really hot day, Bracken finally got hold of the slug-trap, galloped across the lawn, back legs overtaking front legs, straight through the patio doors and did a circuit of the lounge spraying the stale slug-trap mixture all over the carpet and furniture.

I managed to clear up the mess eventually and we still have Bracken. But we do not have slug-traps any more – or hostas.

Elizabeth Brown

Enjoy your meal?

Many years ago we had a young Beagle puppy called
Charlie (the latest is called George). One evening we had
a few friends round for a meal, and eventually, Charlie
flopped, as puppies do, and settled under the table for a
snooze. We enjoyed the meal and imbibed fairly heavily,
and Charlie was as good as gold – not a peep out of
him . . .

When it was time for our guests to leave, one lady got
to her feet, looked for her shoes which she had kicked
off with gay abandon during the meal, put them back on,
lurched unsteadily, tottered a few steps, then fell flat on
her back.

We all thought it was the wine, until the lady spotted
that Charlie had neatly chewed through both heels of her
shoes, leaving little gnarled stumps where the fashionable
stilettos had been – hence no balance! That was a *very*
expensive supper party!

Paddy

Magnificent obsession

My parents had a miniature Yorkshire Terrier, who was
a compulsive thief. This particular morning we sent Minty
upstairs to wake my father who doted on him. My mother
and I were standing at the bottom of the stairs by the front
door talking, when Minty, his beady little eyes gleaming
triumphantly, appeared at the top of the stairs with the
bottom set of Dad's false teeth dangling from his mouth.

Because he was so small, he could not see the stairs
over the teeth and tumbled down, squeaking on contact

with each stair. Then, with his jaws still firmly clenching the teeth, he hit the front door with a thud. Mum and I tried to out-wit him by cutting off his escape and trapping him behind the sofa, but we were no match for this artful dodger who ricocheted off the cushions, sprinted through the kitchen and deftly popped out through the cat-flap.

'Quick,' stammered my mother breathlessly, 'watch to see where he buries them.'

After making three attempts to put us off the trail, Minty finally settled on a spot under the rose bushes.

Half-an-hour later, my father came down, oblivious to the commotion, and asked gummily: 'Doreen, have you seen my teeth?' 'You left them down here last night, dear,' she replied with Oscar-winning normality, and pointed to the hurriedly exhumed and washed teeth! Months later – and only after Dad had had a couple of pints – we told him the truth.

On another occasion Minty's zest for stealing was revived when he spotted a nest of small kittens apparently abandoned under a bush in his garden. One by one he carefully transported the kittens through our cat-flap and into his warm cosy basket in the kitchen. Mother, bleary-eyed, entered and proceeded to go about making breakfast. As she turned and headed for the fridge, small writhings from inside Minty's basket caught the corner of her eye. Suddenly, wide awake, her piercing screams reached the rest of the household who came running convinced she was being murdered.

Dad was the first to arrive on the scene which now comprised Mother standing on top of the worktop, pressed against the wall, shaking and pointing an unsteady finger at Minty's basket. 'Rats . . .' she stammered. Just then, Minty popped in through the cat-flap with the last of his charges dangling from his mouth, followed by the irate mother of the litter.

To this day, Mum still cannot recall how she managed to get up on to the worktop.

Minty went broody after that, so we bought him a couple of small fluffy toys which he alternately mothered, beat up, hid and made love to, depending on his mood!

Vivienne Tregidga

Using plastic!

I had taken my Border Collie, Jason, for an extra long walk over fields, but, getting pushed for time, I came back up the main street.

Jason was on the lead, of course. Suddenly he started barking and tugging so hard, he nearly pulled my arm out of its socket. I couldn't see what was exciting him, but then he came to a halt by a plastic charity dog where much friendly licking and nuzzling took place! Passers-by were in hoots and I felt a right lemon! We didn't live it down for ages.

Judie Wills

What a whiff!

In the mid-1980s, my mother, Joan, and I and my two children lived together with Candy, our little Westie. Each year when we went on holiday, Candy moved into a lovely kennel for the duration. This particular year the usual kennel was closed, so I looked around for another. Having heard horror stories about kennels, I looked very closely at them before choosing one. We duly took Candy to a promising-looking one nearby and trotted off to Bognor.

On arrival home, we immediately went to pick up Candy. Going through the gate, I saw a lovely whiter-than-white mongrel tied to a post, which I patted on the head as I went past. All the other dogs were in a large mesh-enclosed pen barking noisily and looking somewhat dishevelled and dirty.

The kennel lady came out, asked my name, asked me

for the money, then said, pointing to the mongrel tied to the post, 'There's your dog all ready for you.' I said, 'That's not my dog . . .' After some confusion, we started looking in the pen, and I soon saw Candy, as black as a hob, barking madly at me. I pointed her out to the kennel lady who, having nearly passed out with shock and embarrassment, sheepishly went to get her.

Candy smelt indescribably *awful* and looked even worse! I took her out to the car. At the first whiff, my mum nearly fainted, and so did the children in the back. We kept all the windows open all the way home, and I ran Candy straight into the house and up to the bathroom.

When the lady gasped nervously, 'We've bathed the wrong dog . . .', it was the understatement of the year.

Joan Dinsale & Joan Dunn

Customer complaints, this way

During the early 1980s when my then-husband, Michael, and myself ran a small car workshop, we had a wonderful dog called Biggles – a black-and-white Collie/Springer Spaniel – who was a great help in the running of the business!

One afternoon Michael, Biggles, a friend called Ian, and myself were in the office, when a chap who was clearly very miffed about something came storming up the stairs and started to complain bitterly. Michael was busy pacifying him when Biggles suddenly got up from where he had been dozing, went over to the complainant and was sick all over his feet. He then, without a backward glance, returned to his dozing. The stunned silence was followed by stifled giggles.

As the irate customer turned tail and fled, never to be seen again, Ian said: 'I didn't realize you had an assistant in the complaints department!'

Frances Curzons

Mitsi's runner

One morning, intending to take Mitsi, my puppy, for a quick walk on the way to my Keep Fit Class, I grabbed her and put her on the back seat of the car.

At that moment the milkman turned up for his money. After paying him I loaded up the rest of my gear, slammed the boot shut, leapt into the car and shot off to the park for Mitsi's quick walk. On arrival, to my absolute horror, there was no Mitsi!

Distraught, I drove back to the house, thinking all sorts of appalling things like: supposing she had run in the road after me and got knocked down, or tried to follow the car and got lost, etc., etc. When I arrived home, however, there she was sitting on the doorstep, parked between two cats. They, I might add, were solicitously washing her.

I decided she must have nipped out of the car while I was loading it up and chased after the cats. It taught me to check that she was with me before driving off, and it certainly taught Mitsi never to chase cats. She never did after that.

Anon

Feeling peckish!

Our old black Labrador, Anna, frequently opens the fridge when left on her own, helping herself to whatever she fancies. On one occasion we returned to find her sitting very sheepishly in her bed, not wanting to look at us because the fridge door was open, an empty plate was on the kitchen floor, and there was no sign of the roast beef. When she was a puppy, she also ate a pound note which had been left on the table.

We also have a cat who frequently comes into the kitchen, opens the fridge and looks in to see what she fancies.

We now keep a chair in front of the fridge!

Paula Whitehouse

How do *they* do that!

Laddie was a very amiable dog, but he had one particular enemy. We never knew the dog's name, but the owner was called Billy Hooker. We only had to say 'Billy Hooker' and Laddie would go absolutely berserk.

In those days my parents kept a confectioner's shop and we lived 'over the shop' – as all the best people did of course! Anyway, on this particular day, we were all in the upstairs sitting-room with the window wide open. The sunblind was out over the shop window below us. Suddenly we spotted the enemy approaching and naughtily teasing Laddie, shouting: 'Look, Laddie, there's Billy Hooker'.

Before anyone could stop him, Laddie leapt up from his snooze and plunged straight through the open window. Rolling down the sunblind, he got to his feet, and raced off across the market place after Billy Hooker and his dog.

Just then, a very startled man emerged from beneath the sunblind, looked up at the window, and said in a broad Norfolk accent: 'Cor . . . I've heard of it raining cats and dogs afore, but I never thought I'd see it happen!'

Diana Newstead

Muffy-Maid!

I have a black dog, called Muff, who is now fourteen-and-a-half. About ten years ago I was invited to visit a friend for coffee and was told to bring Muff with me. My friend told me to let Muff off her lead, and we chatted away as she pottered happily round the room, nose to the ground, sniffing every inch of the floor – she always likes to investigate new surroundings thoroughly before she sits down.

As we discussed this and that over coffee, we forgot all about Muff, but suddenly heard a pitter-pattering noise coming from overhead, and realized that Muff had found her way upstairs into the main bedroom above the living-room.

My friend assured me that this did not matter in the slightest as she couldn't do any harm. So, we relaxed again and left her to it. Imagine my horror when, some time later, the living-room door was pushed open to reveal Muff, head, top-knot and whiskers, completely smothered and draped in cobwebs.

I don't know who was the most embarrassed, my friend or me. Since then, I have never let Muff go upstairs alone in someone else's house!

Mrs Jackie Thomas

Stick-y customer

Our Old English Sheep-dog was 'king' of thieves, and his particular favourites were bread, cheese and chocolate. On this particular occasion, we were preparing for a family party, and my husband and I went to the supermarket (complete with Barney in the car) to do some last-minute shopping. We piled all the shopping into the back of the car, covered it carefully, and then drove round to the petrol station to fill up.

I was sitting happily listening to the radio when I noticed several people pointing to the back of our car and killing themselves with laughing.

Turning round, I saw Barney polishing off the second of three large sticks of bread. Before I could get to the back of the car, which was now littered in breadcrumbs, he had started on the third. The sight of me, having a tug-of-war with Barney to retrieve the last disappearing stick of bread set the whole forecourt in an uproar. Barney, thanks to his size, won. I lost!

Mrs Kathleen Black

Hair of a dog!

Our Golden Retriever, Magnus, was a compulsive thief. One Christmas I put three pounds of mixed fruit in a bowl to soak overnight in half-a-pint of rum, whisky and brandy.

The next morning, I came down to an empty bowl on the floor and soon spotted one very sick hung-over dog flopped out in his basket. He *looked* hung-over, too. He had very red eyes, and was obviously suffering from a headache that made him cringe at every sound. He spent the entire day staggering outside at frequent intervals to be ill.

On another occasion we located him running along the open slopes of Portsdown Hill, where we were walking him, with a whole crusty loaf in his mouth, which he was busy scoffing while on the run.

Needless to say, we walked on pretending he was not with us.

Mrs Jan Grinham

Bon appétit

Toddy, my eighteen-month-old Cavalier King Charles, digs up stones in the garden and, if he can't crunch them up, swallows them whole.

I wrote to the vet on the *Jimmy Young Show* recently asking his advice, and was told to coat the stones with Tabasco sauce and rebury them. Then, when he swallowed them, Toddy would burn his mouth and mend his ways. Ha-ha!

Toddy duly dug up the stones, sneezed six times, swallowed them, licked his lips, and went back for more.

Bad habit No. 2 is that he always carefully wipes his mouth on the carpet whenever he has finished eating.

Mary Sheppard

How much is it worth?

I had never been very fond of dogs and I still can't bear cats! However, when my next-door neighbour was ill, I offered to do some cleaning for her, even though she had a Spaniel, called Jessica, which she asked me to let out mid-morning. A bit afraid of handling Jessica, I hit upon the idea of opening the garden door and throwing a biscuit outside for her to follow. She did . . . so all was well! However, when I tried the same trick the next week,

CARY 95.

Jessica came and stood on my feet! As she was much heavier than me I couldn't move and was pinned to the floor. Eventually, I managed to twist myself round and reach for the biscuits. I threw one into the garden, but she still didn't move. She just looked at me as if to say 'You'll have to do a lot better than that'. So, I threw several more biscuits, but without success. Finally, I showed her the empty tin. At that point, she grinned, got off my feet, walked casually off into the garden and ran round gobbling up all the biscuits.

Olive Gregson

In the hot seat!

One freezing cold morning in February this year, I was up very early and thought I would pop Shannon, my fourteen-month-old Golden Retriever bitch, into the car and take her for a walk before I went to work.

Leaving my husband and two sons in bed I crept out of the house, not wishing to wake anyone so early, and put Shannon in the car. I started the engine, put the fan-heater on full, then, realizing all the windows were iced up, got out to scrape them, closing the car door in case Shannon jumped out.

As I started to scrape the front window, Shannon climbed into the front of the car and started to jump up and down, obviously thinking all this scraping was a new game. As I started on the driver's side window, Shannon jumped up and down again. Suddenly there was an unmistakable *click*. She had jumped on to a lock and activated the central locking system. I could not believe she had done this. 'Don't panic,' I thought. 'Try all the doors.' I did – they were all well and truly locked. 'Climb through the boot,' I thought. But the boot was locked too.

Now I panicked! Shannon was locked in the car, fan-heater full on, and the engine running!

I decided to let myself into the house and wake my oldest son, but then I realized the house-keys were on the car key-ring, which was in the car!

There was nothing for it, but to bang on the front door. About five minutes later someone inside heard me. By this time several neighbours' lights were on and curtains were twitching.

Out, at last, came both my sons followed by my not-very-happy husband. Then, because we do not have a spare key, they all tried for twenty minutes to get into the car. By now, Shannon was very hot and bothered and definitely wanting to get out, thank you!

When my son eventually got into the car, poor old Shannon jumped out, panting frantically.

By this time I had quite gone off the idea of taking her for an early-morning walk. Exhausted, I went back inside and settled for a cup of hot sweet tea.

Vanessa Cox

Something in the way he moves . . .

My late mother- and father-in-law had a general dealers shop on the outskirts of Jarrow, South Tyneside. During the time they were in the shop, they had a German Pointer called Pax – probably due to the influence of my brother-in-law who is a Benedictine monk.

One summer, my mother-in-law was serving a customer when she was startled by a lady rushing in, crying: 'Mrs . . . Come quick. There's something wrong with your dog . . .'

Outside, the lady pointed to Pax's rear end, and mother-in-law, horrified at what she saw, quickly ushered Pax into the garden at the rear of the shop.

He was walking very strangely and something very odd was hanging out of his hind quarters. My mother-in-law could only watch, horrified, as the 'something' grew longer and longer. Eventually, when the 'something' finally flopped on to the garden path, she identified it as a pair of lady's tights!

Pax, the rascal, had obviously been rummaging in the laundry basket, had somehow devoured the tights, and they were now being returned!

Bob Waugh

Rex's sit-in

We once had a large, male, black Labrador called Rex who was a bit of a sex maniac. Because he was always getting into trouble over girls, and returning wounded, the vet suggested we should have him castrated. Just before we agreed to this, he got into such serious trouble over a girl, he had to stay in hospital for two weeks.

After being neutered, he decided that, from now on, Food would be his Thing. He then became so fat, I decided not to take him out anymore in the car. Rex, aware that our small dog was still going out in the car, clearly thought this was inexcusable discrimination.

One day, noticing that, on return from shopping, I had left the car door open, Rex jumped in and would *not*, for love or food, get out.

I tried everything – including giving in and taking him for a drive. That didn't work either. I made him up a delicious dish of food, but that failed to coax him out. In fact, nothing worked. He just continued his sit-in.

When Bill came home, he, too, took him for a drive. But to no avail! Rex continued his sit-in.

Eventually, we were reduced to opening the two back doors of the car, and while one of us *pushed* the other *pulled*, until, after what seemed forever, we managed to tip him out.

We never left the car door open, unguarded, ever again. As for Rex, he never gave up watching for his second chance.

Eileen Prince

Bed of roses

My daughter, Valerie, although a nurse, makes beautiful celebration cakes and ices them to people's wishes. One bride wanted a three-tier cake with decorative iced roses cascading down from top to bottom.

After a hard day's work at the hospital, Valerie spent a hard day's night making over a hundred roses, which she carefully left on a board in the kitchen.

The next morning, her husband, Chris, a police dog-handler brought his dog home, left him in the garden, and went into the house.

Yes, you've guessed, he left the garden door open. The dog, usually obedient and not usually allowed into the house . . .

By the time Valerie remembered the roses, it was too late – every single one had gone.

Valerie was *not* a happy girl that morning. The dog, on the other hand, lay down happily on his 'bed' of roses, and never stopped licking his lips.

Lily Rabbitts

Lost and found

In March, after fourteen happy years, I had to say goodbye to my best pal, a Golden Setter called Clyde.

About a month ago I went to look at some Golden Setter puppies, and ended up with Clyde Mk II.

One day, Clyde Mk II went missing. Having searched the house from top to bottom twice, I was completely at a loss where to find him.

Then, at long last, I struck lucky. He was curled up fast asleep in the drum of the washing machine.

Donald Fowler

Ginger nutter

Some years ago we 'adopted' a stray greyhound from the RSPCA. His mission in life was to devour everything which was vaguely edible, be it fruit, veg, flesh or fowl, raw or cooked, fresh or decomposing, it mattered not one jot to our Louis.

In our village was a small branch of Lloyds Bank with

very friendly cashiers. I always combined my visits to the bank with Louis' lunch-time 'walkies', and he was regularly treated to a couple of ginger biscuits by the staff who would push the treats under the security screen for him. On one occasion, however, the exchange of a large canvas bag of change meant that the security screen was opened up for a moment. Presumably Louis imagined this to be the entrance to some ginger-nut paradise. Before I could gather my senses, he had sprung from the floor, through the security screen and landed on all fours in the cash scoop. Fortunately I had enough tension on the lead to prevent him completing his trajectory into the lap of the surprised cashier.

Not even the most dog-loving person would relish the sudden descent of a fully grown, ginger-nut-crazed greyhound on to their person during normal banking hours!

Mrs Margaret Stokes

That's mine

When we moved from London to the South-west some years ago, our new neighbours invited us into their house for a cup of tea to welcome us.

Ushered into their kitchen, I was sitting holding a large mug of steaming tea, waiting for it to cool down, when I noticed their mongrel dog had sat down in front of me and was staring mesmerized at the mug in my hand.

'Don't worry about him,' my new neighbour said, 'you've got his mug. He won't move till he gets his.'

Rita

Next, please

I was suffering from a miserable pain in my lower back and having to make regular visits to an osteopath. On this particular occasion, when I arrived, there was, to my great relief, nobody in the waiting room, except for a Dachshund, lying down, head on paws. 'Thank goodness,' I thought, 'I'll be next, and in and out in time to grab a sandwich before returning to the office'.

A few minutes later, the osteopath's voice boomed: 'Muffin. Come on, Muffin. There's a good boy.'

With barely a moment's hesitation, the dog got up and gingerly walked in the direction of the voice.

A few minutes later, when Muffin's mistress appeared from a side-room chat with the receptionist, I learned that the dog was having twice-weekly sessions. He had injured his back jumping over a low wall to greet a passing lady-love!

Barty

'You must give me the recipe . . .'

I had some friends coming over for the evening and decided to try my hand at making a steak and kidney pie. Being a cheat, I bought a tin of steak and kidney from the local shop and popped it in the larder.

On the day, I added mushrooms and onions to the tin of meat and made up some nice thick gravy to give the dish a really authentic home-made taste.

As we sat down to start eating, and enjoy the bottle of wine, I was aware of my dog constantly whining and poking his nose at me. 'Oh, dear,' I apologized to the guests, 'I forgot to feed him. I'll have to do it. He won't give us any peace until I do.'

Now, I have one of those wretched can-openers which, if you do not remove the food label on the tin first, gets the paper blocked in its little wheel and grinds to a halt. For this reason, I always remove labels before attempting to open.

With my dog still nosing me along, I went to the larder to get out his tin of dog food, but, alas, could not find it anywhere. The only tin present, I very soon realized, was the tin of Steak and Kidney. I stood there, like Basil in *Fawlty Towers*, staring in disbelief, saying: 'What have I done? What have I done?'

Still disbelieving, I crossed to the pedal bin, retrieved the label, and, putting on my glasses, read: 'Fine meaty chunks in a rich gravy'. It *was* dog meat. What a bloomer!

As the dog pawed me again, I opened the tin of steak and kidney, thrust it at him, and rushed back into the dining-room to see what was happening. My guests were all blissfully happy, chatting away, eating my pie with great relish. 'Everything okay?' I whimpered. 'Yes, lovely pie. You must give me the recipe,' one of them replied.

There was no escape. I had no choice but to sit down and join them in the eating of my specially prepared pie.

As for the dog . . . suffice it to say, having dined, he slept contentedly for the rest of the evening.

John Adams

Miaows

Milking the milkman dry

My small white cat was absolutely convinced it was a Retriever and constantly staggered home with assorted trophies, such as balls of wool, clothes pegs, bits of paper, and so on and on.

One day I was asking our replacement milkman what had happened to his predecessor, and was told he had had a nervous breakdown. Soon, while spring-cleaning the cat's bed in the broom cupboard, I found out why. Under the dust-sheets, obviously collected on the cat's early-morning rounds, was a pile of crumpled notes bearing messages: 'No milk today.' 'One-dozen eggs, please.' 'Away all next week.' And so on, and so on, and . . .

Please omit my surname in case the milkman or his family read this!

Alison

Pussy galore

We once had a black cat called Mickey. Or, to be more precise, *He had Us*.

After about ten years of his company, I responded to a ring at the door to find a neighbour, from a few doors down, asking if we could do them a favour and feed their cat while they were on holiday. The more we got chatting about their cat and its likes and dislikes, the more it sank in that it was no coincidence that it sounded *exactly* like our cat, Mickey. It was *not* a clone – it was the *same* cat.

All those years, Mickey had eaten heartily at our house, had a good sleep by the fire, then took himself off and had dinner No 2. We would never have cottoned on if our neighbours had not knocked on our door. And Mickey lived for twenty-one years. How many dinners is that . . . ?

Mike Sammes

SK: A lot . . . and half of them were free, Mike!

A mere trifle

I had lovingly prepared a sponge in a bowl for a trifle, put in the sherry and left it to soak in while I went out. On arrival home, I noticed Precious, my cat, looked cross-eyed and groggy. With the exception of a few crumbs, she had eaten the whole sponge.

Julie Rochefort

Loo roll!

My parents were left in charge of my sister's Lilac Point Siamese kitten, Ben, and I got a 'phone call at work from my desperate mother who told me that, in the few seconds it had taken my father to open the door to the loo and lift the lid, Ben had leapt in and gone head-first down the lavatory pan! My father had dragged Ben out by the scruff of his neck, wrapped him in a towel and then collapsed on to the settee!

Knowing how my sister dotes on her pets, I phoned the vet, and told him the tale, but he just could not stop laughing. You see, there was one of those sanitizing 'blue blocks' in the cistern and my father was worried that this would poison Ben. The vet assured me the kitten would come to no harm, and, as he was a Lilac Point Siamese, said he would probably be just a bit more lilac!

Sandie Dennis

Ten out of ten for trying!

When we were all living at home my Mother always bought the Sunday joint on Saturday, cooked it that day, and then put it in the pantry on a marble slab until the next day. My brother John and myself were in our late teens and Saturday night was our favourite night out. John would come home in the early hours and start making something to eat. This would infuriate mother (in bed!) as he always left the pantry door open and inevitably the cat would sneak in and eat the joint.

Having decided enough was enough, a notice was

prepared for pinning to the pantry door the next Saturday night: *Keep the door closed. Meat in pantry.*

The next Saturday, notice duly pinned on door, John rolled home. He made his supper and, yes, he *closed* the pantry door – hurrah. The next morning, when we all came down, where was the cat? He had shut it in the pantry – with the joint.

Barbara Ashworth

And . . . nine out of ten for trying

I have three cats, two of which are big, brawny, superb mousers. The third, Kizzy, is very small and dainty and, to my knowledge, has never caught a mouse in her life. Her greatest achievement, until the occasion of this story, had been catching a few moths.

It was a Sunday morning and I was enjoying an extra hour in bed when I was awakened from my semi-doze by a strange noise which sounded like somebody dragging a metal object over concrete. The noise kept stopping and starting. Eventually, I could bear it no longer. I stumbled downstairs, made my way to the back door, unlocked it and opened it.

There, sitting triumphantly with her 'catch' was my little cat, Kizzy. Her 'catch' was, in fact, a dead mouse in a metal mouse-trap. With great difficulty, she had retrieved the trap from our neighbours' garden, brought it across a wide ditch, and then down our long garden path. Getting through our cat-flap, however, had defeated her.

I just had to give her a hug, and nine-out-of-ten for trying.

Maureen Drennen

Cat burglar

In the 1970s, I had a pet Staffie/Corgi crossbreed named Cymru, and a cat named Sasha – a stray that had adopted my father and me. At the time, I did shift-work and, one afternoon, I woke with a start unsure what had woken me. I had left the radio playing quietly downstairs and knew my father was out for the day, but as I lay gathering my senses I could hear movements. I listened carefully. The sounds were definitely not coming from the radio, but from the spare room at the end of the passage.

With thoughts of intruders looming large – there had been a spate of daytime break-ins recently – I crept as silently as I could to my half-opened bedroom door. I am a born coward, but I was concerned for Cymru and Sasha whom I had left sleeping soundly in the living-room. As I listened nervously, another bumping scraping sound came from the spare room. I peered out into the passage and saw Cymru sitting perfectly still by the spare-room door staring intently inside as if she were watching something. The hairs on the back of my neck stood on end – intruders! Another sound came from the room, and, at that moment, Cymru, obviously pleased, tail-wagging, pushed open the door and entered. Realizing by now that it must be Sasha in the room, I breathed a deep sigh of relief and went to see what they were up to. As I approached I heard a 'splat' noise and, a few seconds later, another 'splat'. I crept up to the door and looked in.

Sasha was on top of a cupboard where I kept a tray of fresh eggs that a friend brought me from her own chickens every other week. As I stood watching, she carefully hooked another egg from the tray with her paw, tapped it to the edge of the cupboard, then edged it over to join its shattered companions on the floor where Cymru was now sitting patiently waiting. 'Splat'! When this egg landed, Sasha jumped down and both animals fell to, eating the raw eggs (and shells!) with great enjoyment.

At last, the mystery of the missing eggs was solved (I had earlier on accused my father of using (or breaking) eggs without telling me).

When I pushed open the spare-room door, saying loudly, 'What are you two up to?', two guilty faces, dripping raw egg, looked up at me startled. Then Sasha, with great dignity, stalked past me and made her way, tail swishing downstairs. Cymru, always a glutton, snatched a last mouthful of shell and then scampered past me, crunching away like mad. By the time I got downstairs they were both pretending to be asleep in their usual places on opposite sides of the living-room.

Miss Barbara E. Owen

Stray cat

Oh, what unhappy twist of fate
Has brought you homeless to my gate?
The gate where once another stood
To beg for shelter, warmth and food.
For from that day I ceased to be
The master of my destiny.

While he, with purr and velvet paw
Became within my house, The Law.
He scratched the furniture and shed,
And claimed the middle of my bed.
He ruled in arrogance and pride,
And broke my heart the day he died.

So if you really think, Oh Cat,
I'd willingly relive all that
Because you come, forlorn and thin
Well . . . don't just stand there . . . come on in!

Francis Witham

Pets wanted

My dear mother, now in her late seventies, fainted in Hammersmith Post Office and was promptly whipped off by ambulance to nearby Charing Cross Hospital. My mother has an irrational fear of hospitals and as soon as she was able, and in spite of all the entreaties of the staff, she discharged herself, giving as the reason the totally fictitious need to 'feed her cat and three kittens' shut up at home.

Greatly concerned for her well-being, the hospital telephoned my brother to ask him to get mother back to them without delay after she had 'fed her pets'. Not wishing to expose his mother in a lie, he helpfully confirmed that she would, of course, be very worried about her 'two little dogs'.

Maggie Ferrari

Perfect timing

Some years ago, when we lived in Macclesfield, we invited a couple in the next street for dinner one night. Things went well: Chanette being a great cook had done us proud, and the three-course banquet was greatly appreciated by all.

After the meal, we adjourned to the easy chairs, and brandies, and generally chatted, as you do. The couple told us about their favourite Sunday lunch – leg-of-lamb roast, with garlic, and the usual vegetables. Apparently, on one occasion, after carving the lamb, and dishing up the veggies, they had left the lamb on the window ledge to cool while they set about the first course in the dining-room. Suddenly the sound of breaking crockery alerted them, and, upon entering the kitchen, they caught sight of an enormous black cat, with leg-of-lamb, disappearing through the window – never to be seen again.

It was at this point in the tale, when Tiddles, our rather large adventurous cat, woke up, thudded downstairs on her leaden feet and made her appearance in the lounge.

Simultaneously our guests pointed at Tiddles, and, in perfect harmony, screamed 'That's the cat . . .'

As we all know, animals have a great sense of timing, and Tiddles certainly proved that point, that night!

Brian Burgess

In the pink!

My friend has a cat called Kitty. When I write to her using a pink envelope, Kitty hooks out the 'pinkie' from the rest of the mail and sits on it. When I run out of pink envelopes and use blue, cream or white envelopes, she is not in the slightest bit interested. So, just imagine three OAPs scouring the shops of Farnham, Midhurst and Chichester for pink envelopes to please a cat!

Mrs Sylvia Pett

Wandering star!

We live on a retirement complex of sixty flats and one of our rules is 'no pets'. One pretty black-and-white cat, however, cares nothing for rules and regularly strolls around the complex en route to her 'wash room' on a bit of waste ground nearby.

All the residents know her, and enjoy stroking her as she goes by. She sits very demurely while the ladies stroke her, but rolls over, like a wanton hussy! on her back, offering her fluffy white tummy to the men.

She often enjoys sitting in our porch soaking up the sun during the day, but we never saw her after dark, until one bitterly cold night we found her sleeping there. Worried that maybe her owners had gone away and deserted her, we took her in (just for the night you understand) until we could find out where she lived. She immediately snuggled down on my husband's lap, purring and looking very smug.

Next day, we discovered that, far from being homeless or deserted, she lived in a lovely home with nice people and two other cats, both younger than she was. Mitzi, as we now know she is called, is an elderly cat and it seems she prefers to be in elderly company. Her young 'mum' told us that, in the last five years, she has tried to move in with no less than five other elderly residents and that she has perfected her lost-and-hungry look. Just for the moment, we were her favourites so, with her owner's consent, she continued to sit on our porch all day and, once a day, my husband would walk her back to her house, with Mitzi trotting behind him like a dog. On arrival, she would pop in through the cat-flap, grant her owners half-an-hour of her time, then return to our porch. We have all heard of 'Pat' dogs, but this 'Stroke' cat certainly gives us all a lot of pleasure.

Yesterday, we didn't see much of her. Then, as the district nurse was passing, she called out 'If you are looking for Mitzi, she is sitting with Rose in her flat'. So, perhaps, we have had our turn. But we do hope she will still look in when passing. She probably knows Rose isn't too well, and that she needs her company more than we do at the moment.

Joyce Gillham

Come home, Choky

My son and his family live in a small Close where most of the gardens are open plan, and most of the houses have cat-flaps. My son had two tabby cats, a brother and sister called Ludvig and Choky, who were totally inseparable – that is, until the new baby arrived and Choky decided to leave home and move in with a family further down the Close.

After many attempts to get her to return – and a lot of heart-searching – it was decided to let her remain there. A few days passed and then, one morning on his way to the garage, Simon noticed something rather familiar (his pants) on the pavement. With a somewhat red face he picked them up, popped them into the hall, and then went off to work with just a passing thought.

That evening his wife asked how a strange bra came to be on the hall carpet. Simon denied all knowledge, of course. Next day he found a pair of his socks on the lawn, followed by various other items of underwear as the week progressed. Then, on the Saturday morning, Choky's new mum came to the house with a small pile of clean clothing that she had kindly washed after Ludvig had carried it in his mouth along the road and through the cat-flap – sometimes dropping items on the way.

We decided that he was so confused by his sister now living in a different house that he was slowly moving the old house to her! Everything eventually calmed down, and the only thing that Ludvig takes to our neighbours now is the occasional mouse. As long as he takes it to Choky and not from her to us, that's okay with us!

Anon

Toad in the hall

I have two cats. One is a regular hunter, doing what comes naturally. The other one, Meggy, is much gentler. She likes to stalk, catch and bring indoors, but does not kill. On one occasion the family were out and I thought I would have a luxurious bath, lots of hot water and a book. I was wallowing happily when I heard a loud squeal. I froze. What on earth was it? Silence. Then another squeal.

I leapt out of the bath, donned a skimpy bath-towel and rushed downstairs thinking that perhaps one of the cats had been hurt in some way. But, oh no. Meggy had brought in the most enormous toad who was lying on the hall carpet, on his back, squealing his head off. When I approached him he played dead, deflating unbelievably. I picked him up and examined him to make sure he had not been hurt and then gently ran him under the tap. This obviously revived him and he hopped off quite happily when I put him back into the deepest jungle part of the garden.

On another occasion I 'lost' a mouse in the hall. Meggy had brought it in, but it managed to escape into the minutest of cracks and I just couldn't find it. I did a couple of days later, though – in my garden shoes when I went to put them on!

Gill Turner

Fair catch!

When I was ten, we had a lively black-and-white cat, called Monty, who loved to sit on top of our wireless set, because of the warmth. As the wireless was on a shelf, this also gave him a commanding view of the room.

The Insurance Man (who we were fairly sure was bald and wore a toupee) used to call every Friday night. One evening when he arrived, Monty, in very skittish mood, had retreated to his usual place atop the wireless from whence he glared down at everyone. The Insurance Man's head bobbed around as he talked, and Monty, seeing the animated toupee, crouched menacingly and then leapt! The toupee was off in a trice, and Monty retreated upstairs with it, hiding under a bed and growling fiercely, as cats do, when anyone tries to deprive them of their prize.

Eventually Monty was lured from his retreat with a plate of fish, and our Insurance Man was able to continue his round with his toupee – but not his dignity – restored. Fortunately, he moved to another district a few months later.

Graeme and Elizabeth Young

A budding make-up artiste?

When my daughter, Zoe, was about three, we had visitors to dinner – her Aunt and Uncle. After the meal, Zoe left the table and, while we were chatting, things were very quiet elsewhere! We suddenly realized this and called out 'Zoe, what are you doing?' As there was no response, we thought it prudent to investigate.

Walking into our lounge, we found that she had plundered her Aunt's handbag of all its goodies, had cut all the whiskers off Sandy, our ginger tom – and, for good measure, had smothered him, herself, the settee and the carpet with lipstick.

We still do not know how she managed to hold the cat still and cut off all his whiskers, but whiskerless he was for a very long time.

Carole Mayho

Very fishy!

In the early 1930s I lived with my mother in a bed-sit in London. One Sunday my aunt and uncle were coming to tea, and, as a special treat, my mother had bought my uncle a pint of shrimps, and left them in the bag on the draining board while we walked to meet our visitors.

When we returned for tea, there were no shrimps – no bag – no nothing. We were all mystified, and, as at the time, we had a pet kitten we all looked very suspiciously at her. I cannot remember now what we had for tea, but it certainly wasn't shrimps. Over the next week, however, the shrimps re-appeared – under rugs, behind curtains, in the beds, under pillows and behind cushions. You name it, the kitten had hidden one there – even the rolled-up bag in which the shrimps had been. For days, there was a very fishy smell, and this was in the days when air-fresheners did not exist!

Mrs B. J. Tye

A case of mistaken identity

We have always had several cats and, two years ago, new neighbours and their two cats moved into the house backing on to ours. One of their cats – Willow – is a very beautiful Oriental cat, but a terrible bully. He got into the habit of coming into our house and chasing our three cats. One of them, Dougal, had always been a bit of a wimp (a coward, to be honest) and Willow used to pick on him in particular. It got to the stage where there was open warfare under our bed in the early hours with a lot of bad feline language – growls and appalling threats – and Dougal became more and more neurotic.

We regularly chased Willow out and tried various means of discouraging him, including several nights with me shouting phrases such as: 'Will you get out right now.' 'Don't you *dare* come back in here again.' 'Your behaviour is *absolutely* disgraceful.' '*GET OUT NOW*' . . . etc.

Then my long-suffering husband pointed out that, as no names were ever mentioned, it was very possible that the neighbours were getting the wrong end of the stick and that was why he was getting such very strange looks.

    Eileen Hodder

Picture this

Some years ago, my husband, an ardent 'Western' viewer, settled himself down for two hours of vintage John Wayne, with, as always, the company of our cat, Archie, draped in his favourite spot across the top of the TV.

On this occasion, without any warning, Archie suddenly deposited the contents of his stomach all over the screen – and, yes, into the works at the back. Everything stopped and went silent – except for the unprintable expletives from my husband.

At that time we rented our TV, and the following morning I phoned the rental firm and asked for an engineer to call. 'What seems to be the trouble?' said a robotic voice. 'My cat has been sick in the telly,' I replied. About two minutes passed, then a slightly more interested voice said: 'We haven't come across this problem before. Do you have a picture?'

Needless to say we required a new TV and, if my husband had had his way, a new cat.

Pat Williams

Teacher's pet

Last year my husband, a gardener, came across a tiny abandoned kitten which, much to the delight of our daughter, Beth, aged five, he brought home. Unfortunately the kitten, which Beth named Sooty, only survived for three days.

Trying to convert a very sad situation into a positive experience, we decided to have a garden burial and a prayer, explaining to Beth that Sooty had left his body behind and gone to heaven.

As we stood over the grave Beth remarked how she would have liked to take Sooty to school to show the class. 'You can't take kittens to school Beth,' I said, 'they would run away.' To which she replied, 'No, mummy. Not if it was dead. Hannah brought a starfish last week and that was dead.'

One wonders how teachers cope with what's presented for the nature table!

Margaret Durkin

Wanted – for questioning . . .

We have two cats, Holly and Ivy. They are black-and-white and Holly looks as if she is wearing a balaclava. 'She looks like a cat-burglar,' I once said, not knowing how prophetic a statement that was.

About eight months ago, Holly appeared through the cat-flap with a child's sock dangling from her mouth. She dropped the sock at my feet and gave a smug chirp (have you noticed how many cats don't actually meow?).

More swag soon followed and, over the ensuing weeks, a collection of odd socks and gloves appeared, often with clothes pegs still attached, so we had some idea where she was getting the items. She then stepped up her villainy and two pairs of men's underpants were donated to the household. The next item to arrive was a pink bra, size 34B. Then it was knickers – first a pair of cotton briefs, then some lacy nylon ones.

Once the knickers appeared, I thought it wise to advise the police, just in case anyone else should become a suspect. Needless to say, my call was greeted with some scepticism at first, then muffled laughter, then the suggestion that I should bring her along to the police station for paw-printing.

    David Smith

SK: Any dawn patroller lost a size 34B rose pink . . .

Take that, you . . .

About three years ago, in the middle of summer, during a very hot spell when very little night-clothing was being

worn, our cat was having a howling match about two a.m., beneath our bedroom window. My husband, not wearing much – in view of the hot weather – got up, went down and out into the garden to grab the cat.

Meanwhile, not realizing he had got out of bed, I, too, got up, went to the bathroom, filled a container with cold water, carried it back, and threw it out of the window at the precise moment my husband made a wild grab at the cat. The cat ran off, the security light came on, and my husband, drenched in cold water, stood illuminated by the light.

We are still together, but now keep a loaded water pistol on the windowsill.

Mrs M. Messham

Bewitched, bothered and . . .

A few weeks ago, after trying unsuccessfully to get my cat, William, in, my Mum went to bed at eleven o'clock. Half-an-hour later we were all woken by the doorbell. We rushed downstairs to find two neighbours standing there. Apparently, William was in the kitchen of their elderly neighbour making very loud mewing noises. So Mum rushed along the road in her nightdress to find a lost terrified William crouched in the corner of the work surface.

After many apologies about William's behaviour – and the brown mess he had made! – Mum set off home. To add to her embarrassment, as she walked back down the road carrying William, a pizza boy was delivering a pizza to another neighbour. I wonder what they all thought

Mum was doing . . . out at midnight, in her nightdress, carrying a cat – but no broomstick in sight!

Kate Leslie (ten years old)

Oh, no, here she comes again . . .

I have a black-and-white moggy, called Pollyanna. To get me out of bed she reaches the top of the door, via book-case, and then jumps right on me. If that doesn't work, she rattles the Venetian blind until I can't stand it a moment longer and simply have to get up.

When I am writing (like now) I have to use two pens as she chews the end of the one I'm using. Eventually, I give her that pen and try to get my letter finished with the other before she realizes she's been conned, and comes back for that one, too.

When I'm typing, she either sits on the keys which causes havoc as the machine is electric, or tries to drag the paper out.

My balls of knitting wool disappear like magic or, alternatively, I come to a very sudden stop where she has nibbled through the yarn.

Oh, no, here she comes!

She plays hide-and-seek (which has to be seen to be believed). But the one antic that astonishes people the most is when she carries Squeak, the hamster, around in her mouth like a kitten.

Kath Brodie

Stuck up!

Some years ago we had a cat. One morning, washing up after breakfast, I heard a very loud tap at the door, but low down almost at floor level. On opening the door, there was our cat with a jam-jar stuck over his head. How it happened we shall never know, but wasn't he clever to come home and knock at the door. Suffice it to say, we managed to get his head out without breaking the jam-jar, or hurting him.

Evelyn Veal

Joy rider!

On April 21 I bought a brand new car and on April 22 went away, leaving the car locked securely in my garage. About 4.30 a.m., on the Sunday morning of our return home, I was woken by a loud metallic crash and rushed from the bed to the window expecting to see someone trying to steal the car. But the garage door was closed and there was no sign of an intruder. Puzzled, I went back to bed, thinking I had heard someone else's metal garage door.

Later in the morning I went to the garage to take the new car out. There, resting upside-down on top of the car, was a very large, red plastic, bakers' tray which had been stored for years on the beams supporting the up-and-over garage door. The roof of the car was full of dents; the garage window was slightly ajar.

We have two cats, and the black female – one of nature's indefatigable hunters – slunk guiltily away from me. Then I realized what had happened. A bird had flown into the garage while being chased by the cat. The cat had squeezed through the gap in the window and leapt on to the car roof. The bird had perched on the edge of the bakers' tray and the cat had jumped after it, landing on the edge of the tray, which, of course, then toppled over on to the new car. The loud crash had no doubt terrified both creatures who had fled out of the window by the time I looked out.

The Insurance Claim form read: Who do you blame? My answer: the Cat! It cost over £200 to repair the car-roof, and I had hardly driven it.

Johnne Abrams

A real cool cat

Our late lamented Merlin – a large ginger cat – allowed us to share his home for eighteen years. He died last year and we still miss him.

We live in a second-floor flat so he was unable to go out, but he found his exercise and entertainment in other ways. In his early days (while we were out at work) he managed the following:

1. Blocking the waste-disposal unit with one of his silver paper balls which he loved pushing into or under any inviting opening.
2. Flooding the flat below by disconnecting the washing-machine hose and leaving it on the floor.
3. Pulling down one of the curtains and its rail (well, he weighed over a stone at his heaviest and was an accomplished curtain climber until a few weeks before his death).

4. Inventing a game called 'goodnight Merlin'. This started by accident one night when I switched off the light in the sitting-room, and started to walk out of the room saying 'goodnight Merlin' as I went. There was a thunder of paws (yes, he was extremely heavy-footed – we could always hear him coming even on carpets), and he shot across my path into the doorway. I wasn't sure what I was supposed to do, but he quickly showed me. Every time I said 'goodnight Merlin' and started walking, he would rush from one side of the room to the other – and so a nightly game was established. His one rule – the light had to be off in the sitting-room, but on in the hall!

Gay Berenzweig

Very fetching!

When I came into the kitchen to find bright yellow feathers covering the floor, I thought my cat, Jenny, had caught an exotic bird. Thankfully, it was only a feather duster, but where had it come from? I had never bought a feather duster.

Periodically, after that, Jenny would arrive home with one in her mouth. Eventually I traced the source . . . along the main road, through automatic doors, past J. Sainsbury, and into the shopping mall! There, outside the cane shop, was a basket of feather dusters! Some friends, who worked in Sainsbury's, later told us they had witnessed Jenny trotting back along the main road with a feather duster! Shamefully, I did not offer to pay for the dusters, but, from then on, I made sure she had her own supply.

When we moved into the country she took up fishing – jumping into a neighbour's pond and bringing home her catch. I would then put the catch in a bucket and return it. To his credit, the neighbour was never cross. 'She always comes to help me feed the fish, you know,' he said calmly. 'She is such a sweetie'. Not the word I would use for her!

Sadly, Jenny has long since gone to pussy-cat heaven – she lost while playing a game of 'chicken' with a tipper truck.

Sue Salt

A likely tail!

Our cat, Dusty, is a friendly affectionate animal, intelligent too, and visitors and friends alike have endorsed this reputation. A few days ago we were both disappointed to learn from a neighbour that he had been acting as a bully towards two cats owned by another neighbour. He had also been seen getting through their electronic cat-flap, which should have thwarted him!

The mystery of this apparent sleight of paw was solved the following day when the owner of the cats revealed that Dusty had been seen getting through the flap by clamping his teeth over the tail of one of the cats and proceeding in tandem. So much for Dusty's reputation – he was not only a bully, but a pretty sharp cat burglar.

Ron Cooper

Anyone for pheasant?

If our cat Delphi could talk, she probably wouldn't even speak to the sort of people she has condescended to live with for her fifteen summers.

When she was a lithe Siamese-kittenish one-year-old, I fitted a cat-flap to the kitchen door to let her come and go at will. One Saturday morning, my wife, Sue, and I were attracted by sounds of scuffling at the flap and went to see what the problem might be. There was Delphi, half-way through the flap, struggling to pull a twice-her-size pheasant through after her.

Just where the pheasant had come from we had no idea but, as we live near a field and the bird was quite cold, we assumed she must have picked it up from there. Fearing

that it might have died from poisoning we reluctantly put it deep in the dustbin and firmly put the lid on.

Minutes later . . . there was more scuffling at the cat-flap. On investigation, we found the wretched cat back again with the bird. How on earth had she got into the dustbin? Risking life and limb, we again dragged the pheasant from an exceedingly angry cat, opened the bin . . . only to find the first bird still in place!

Our puzzlement over the incident lasted for several months until the day a neighbour was overheard at a party, describing how thieves had broken into his garage and stolen a brace of pheasants.

Obviously a cat-burglar!

Ray G. Davies

One for the road

Morticia was a black-and-white, long-haired moggie plucked from the centre of a very busy main road in 1983. From the moment she arrived at our house, she made her mark. The food that eight-out-of-ten cats prefer was *not* to her taste – she would only eat tuna, pilchards, evaporated milk and grated cheese, plus the odd dish of biscuits.

During the warm weather of her first summer with us, Morticia decided to move into the garage (which we obligingly fitted with a cat-flap). Every morning and evening, as she refused to come inside, the food had to be taken out to her. Gradually, however, she started disappearing for longer and longer, and would only stand on the doorstep and look in the kitchen. I put a tag on her collar asking if she was visiting anyone or being fed – but no reply came in the six-week trial we gave this idea. The longest trip was thirteen days and we never found out where she went during this time.

We had regular sightings of her around the village, and one day she came home dragging a whole chicken leg that had been cooked and skinned and was obviously very fresh – not something rummaged out of a dustbin. By the time our animals had finished with it, there was only a grease-spot left on the path. We never discovered whose meal was missing the main ingredient.

The following summer, fish and moorhen chicks started to arrive through the cat-flap. Eventually, we discovered a lovely couple with a magnificent garden and a very generous-sized 'pond' (that term being an understatement), well stocked with fish and inhabited by moorhens. Most of the chicks ended up in our house. Sometimes they just appeared from behind furniture after having been brought in while we were out at work – they were always returned a.s.a.p. Fortunately the owners of the 'pond' were of the opinion that Morticia was only doing what came naturally.

In the garden next door to the 'pond' rats had been discovered – the Council could not put poison down as the run could not be found so Morticia decided to clear them out – to our kitchen! We think she started off with Granddad and worked her way through eight rats in ten days – seven live and the smallest one deceased. We had to buy a rat trap and had the awful job of dealing with the results. Some got behind the kitchen units and, one afternoon, when I was writing at the table I could hear a rat running up and down the back of the fridge. I had a peep and the cheeky creature was stealing a biscuit out of the cats' dish, which it then took behind the fridge and I could hear crunch, crunch, crunch. A very cold shiver went down my spine.

Sadly, one day Morticia came in looking very sick indeed, and was taken to the vet and gently released from her suffering. We had more words of condolence from residents of the village whose gardens she used to pass through than if we had lost a relative. One elderly spinster said she would miss her so much and could we train another one to visit her! We got to know many people through Morticia – I was hardly ever known by my name but as Morticia's mother and my mother as Morticia's grandmother! Such was her 'dumb' power of communication.

We miss her greatly, but are very grateful for the years she had with us when she could so easily have met her demise in 1983.

Elaine Pittaway

Thanks for everything

Every summer, during our annual holiday, my next-door neighbour, Avril, would very kindly look after our cat by feeding her every day, leaving a tiny window open during the day and closing it at night. On our return the cat was always eager to meet us, except for this time, so I went next door to see if anything had happened. 'No,' Avril replied, 'I fed her this morning.' We started to unpack the car, when Avril called round to say her Sunday roast, which she had left to thaw, had disappeared – all 3 lbs of it. I knew our cat was a thief, and that anything she stole was always dragged under our bed, so I immediately went to look.

Sure enough, there she was, still gnawing her way through the joint. She must have dragged it from Avril's kitchen, under the hedge, up through the little window and across our floors. What a thank-you for a person who had so kindly looked after her for two weeks!

Patricia Maxwell

Des res

Butch and Sylvia are two feral moggies who made their home in my garden shed. Last autumn a fox managed to get into the shed via the puss-flap, by-passed Butch and Sylvia's sleeping box, and a bit of a fracas then ensued. Needless to say, Butch and Sylvia were not too keen on going into the shed after that.

As they're both old and suffer from rheumatism I was at my wits end this winter wondering how to give them some shelter other than my open porch. I tried so hard to get them into the house and although Butch loved to come in and sit by the radiator, Sylvia, his other half, steadfastly refused. He is so loyal to her that, after about an hour indoors, he would miaow to go out to be with her on the cold doorstep. I felt dreadful when I locked the front door at night, knowing that all they had for a bed was a wet doormat.

When gale-force weather arrived, I decided enough was enough and set about making them a little house which they could easily defend. So, out came the carpentry kit, a sheet of 8 x 4 chipboard, a roll of roofing felt, and a puss-flap. First, I measured Rosie, my indoor moggie, multiplied her by two and marked out the measurements on the chipboard. So far so good. I beavered away in my study for three days. All I can say is this – it came up a bit bigger than the 'pattern' and I could not get the darned thing out of the study door! In the end I had to remove the roof of the cat house before my dad and I – very nearly getting a hernia in the process – eventually managed to squeeze it out.

We put the house on breeze-blocks in the front garden and, to my absolute delight, they moved in about an hour later. Since then, they have rarely ventured out except for meals. I added three layers of blankets and they are even more snug now than they were in the shed.

When it came to choosing a name for the des.res., I thought I could do no better than call it *The Snug*. Come the summer, I am going to plant some pussy pots (catnip) in their front garden. I'm not sure about a picket fence, though.

Sue Costello

Wanna spend a penny, Mum

Morven, my cat, and I are both Glasgow born and bred, and used to travel north frequently to visit our respective mothers. A 350-mile journey is quite long for both driver and cat, so we would regularly stop at service stations along the way. Out we would get to stretch our legs – Morven safely attached to a collar and lead.

On one such occasion, Morven seemed more agitated than usual and I guessed he had need of the 'facilities'. So on went his collar and lead, and I lifted him out. No sooner had his paws touched the ground, than he was off – racing across the car-park with me in hot pursuit at the end of my ten-foot length of string. With unerring instinct he made straight for the 'Ladies', and I only caught up with him when he stopped with his little face pressed under the three-inch gap at the foot of a cubicle door!

I didn't wait to observe the reaction of the occupant,

but called Morven to order and showed him the grass. I was just *very* thankful he had not chosen the 'Gents'!

    Eileen Edward

Not for the pot!

When my son Joe was about four years old, Tom the pigman (he breeds pigs) offered us a guinea-pig. Joe and my daughter Vicky were thrilled to bits and duly went to choose their pet. Having got the guinea-pig tucked up safely in her hutch, Joe said nervously 'This one won't end up in the freezer, will it?'

    Mrs Chris Farmiloe

SK: Aagh . . .

Stuntcat Susie

Susie was a beautiful, long-haired, black-and-white cat – white front and legs, black body with mainly white face, but black from her forehead upwards. Her eyes, heavily black-lined, looked as though she had overdone the make-up, and her black ears were lined with white tufts.

We had two fireside wing chairs, facing each other. Susie would wait until a visitor was settled in one, then run up the back of the chair, hang on with one front paw and tap the visitor's head with the other paw. All the person sitting opposite would see, would be a flash of black ears and sparkling eyes together with a swiping white paw. She would then drop down and run off at break-neck speed.

As these were the days of carpet squares and rugs rather than fitted carpets, these chairs were placed on polished linoleum. When bored, Susie would lie under a chair, catching hold of the underside with her claws, and then proceed to slide herself backwards and forwards on the linoleum until she had worked up to a speed when she could let go and come whizzing out across the floor on her back with her legs raised upwards. Visitors, not knowing she was there, would be startled to see this upturned cat sliding across the floor. When she came to a halt, she would get up, go back and do it all over again. Needless to say, the undersides and backs of the chairs became rather tattered – not to mention the cat!

Doreen Foskett

Super trifle, Mum

This incident occurred about fifteen years ago during the dreaded Christmas visitation of the Three Elderly Aunts from Hell. Their great treat was the sherry trifle I always made for them and, on this occasion, just before serving it I took it out of the fridge to sprinkle on the decoration. Before I could do this, however, a crisis occurred in the dining-room and I left the trifle on the worktop completely forgetting the presence of my two then-young Devon Rex cats who had been banished to the kitchen because the Three Aunts considered cats in general – and mine in particular – to be vermin. Devon Rex cats are notoriously greedy and will eat practically anything, particularly if they can steal it . . .

Moments later, I returned to the kitchen to find them, yes, licking the cream from the trifle, and one with his paw actually *in* the dish to hold it steady! My initial horror turned to amusement – call my darlings vermin, would they? Right! I scraped off what was left of the cream, completely removed the 'pawed' section and jiggled everything around before putting on fresh cream and the decorations. I then called my husband into the kitchen and instructed him to *refuse* the trifle at lunch. 'Why?' he asked suspiciously, looking first at me, then at the smug cats. '*What* have *they* done now?' 'Nothing!' I lied. 'It's just that the aunts are bound to want second helpings and, if we have any, there won't be enough.' Far from convinced, he followed me back to the dining-room. Second helpings were indeed requested and, shortly after lunch, the aunts were returned home.

I awoke at 3.30 a.m., consumed with guilt. How could I have done such a thing. I had awful visions of The Three Aunts being admitted to Intensive Care suffering from food poisoning, the Public Health Department knocking at my door demanding samples of everything they had eaten the previous day, swiftly followed by the police coming to arrest me etc., etc. There was no more sleep for me that night.

It seemed a lifetime until 9.30 a.m., the earliest I dared telephone, but my fears were groundless. All three were in perfect health and 'looking forward to next year, dear', which was more than I was. As for the cats . . .

Helen

A likely tail!

Sam, our English Bull Terrier, was a very lovable dog, but very dense! When he was a pup, he could not understand why our cat, Spooky, did not want his tail-end sniffed and inspected. Every day, we were treated to a black streak of a cat scooting across a room with a brown barrel of a dog lumbering and snorting in hot pursuit.

One fine day, Dad decided that he would finish the painting of our bay windows. He had finished the inside woodwork, and was working on the outside of the sitting-room window, when he heard the usual kerfuffle that occurred whenever Sam decided Spooky's tail-end needed inspecting.

The usual thunder of hooves followed as Spooky scooted down the corridor from the kitchen, closely followed by Sam. The pair raced into the sitting-room, and Spooky jumped on to the back of the settee. Sam, however, was determined that, this time, he was going to have his wicked way, and ran up the sofa as well. The settee fell over and Spooky leapt for the safety of the open window . . .

Dad could only stand aghast, brush in hand, as our black cat leapt towards him, landed on the newly painted window ledge, slipped towards him with all the grace of Torvill and Dean, hit the bottom of the window and did a neat head-roll into the two-and-a-half litre tin of high-gloss white paint hanging from the window brace.

For a cat covered from head to foot with sticky, dripping, horrible-smelling yucky stuff, Spooky took it very calmly. He was very cool, calm and collected as Dad pulled him out, wiped his dripping face and scraped most of the paint back into the tin. He also sat quietly in the sink while Dad washed him twice in white spirit to get the paint off. He radiated peace and tranquillity as he was rinsed twice in detergent to get the white spirit off. It was only as he was being rinsed with clean water to remove the detergent that Spooky decided *That Was IT*. Doing a very impressive impersonation of a Christmas tree, he took off into the garden leaving a trail of diluted paint, white spirit and detergent behind him.

He emerged two days later, as clean as a new pin. He had obviously spent the entire time cleaning himself. After that he never ran away from Sam again, preferring to stand and fight and give him a bloody nose instead – and we *always* shut the door when decorating.

Adrian Kirkup

Houdini

Tiffany Dell, our chocolate-coloured Burmese, has taught herself how to open closed doors. When we turn out the lights, she jumps up and puts them back on again. We carefully shut her out of the bedroom only to find her, sooner or later, sleeping peacefully in the middle of the bed. We have put child-proof locks on the fridge and cupboard doors, but just know she's very busy working those out.

However hard we try to stay ahead, she pops up just anywhere when we are least expecting her. At the moment this includes the hen-house, plus descending in a very sudden pounce right in the middle of the other fourteen cats when they are snugly sleeping in front of the boiler.

She's a nightmare for all of us, but, despite all her mischief, we still love her.

Rozina Hill

Making a splash

Molly, my neighbour, was walking up and down her garden path urgently calling her budgie. Just minutes before I had picked up a large blue feather from my kitchen floor, examined it, frowned puzzled, and dismissed it, until I heard Molly . . .

With 'cap' in hand (or rather feather) I took it to Molly to identify it. It appears that our cat, Splash, had got through Molly's pantry window, walked through the kitchen into the lounge and removed the blue budgie from its cage (door closed). There was no sign of a struggle – not even feathers around the cage. As you can imagine I felt awful, but could only offer to get Molly another budgie.

Georgina Findlay

Best of pals

Fluff, a long-haired ginger tom, strayed into our Close one day and completely won the heart of our neighbour, Dave, who always alleged he hated cats.

Fluff, obviously a conservationist who believed in recycling, would come into our garden, drink copiously from the birdbath, then step into it and urinate.

He then started keeping all the other cats and dogs at bay, and once chased a yelping Golden Retriever out of its own Close.

When we acquired a kitten, named Biniou, Fluff took it upon himself to be his guide and mentor. He taught Biniou how to climb on to neighbours' roofs, but didn't show him how to get down. Consequently, most often after dark, we would hear Biniou calling 'Help. Help,' and I would have to get a ladder out and climb up to the roof. Often by the time I got there, he would have moved to the other side of the roof, still yelling.

At sixteen, thank goodness, he no longer does this, but I have often thought how very lucky I was not to have been arrested or pushed off the ladder by some frightened or irate home-owner!

Among his other talents, Fluff could beg for titbits just like a dog. In the summer, when our bedroom window was left open at night, he would creep in to sleep on our bed, and still be there in the morning. When his 'parents' were away on holiday, he would move in with us. But, as soon as he heard their car enter the Close, he would be off, without a backward glance, to rejoin them.

John and Jill Funnell

Mousey-mousey

Our cat's a very tidy methodical cat. She brings in mice and eats them in the shower basin. If she is not hungry, she deposits the mouse (unharmed) in the bath, and, often when I go into the bathroom in the morning, I find the mouse hunched up, trying to hide itself in the plug-hole. Poor me, poor mice!

Angela Kellie

Rude awakenings

Six weeks ago, Murphy, our cat, was hit by a car and badly injured. Our skilful vet pieced his broken bones together with wire and pins and we had to keep him caged.

Two weeks later, much improved, he was allowed out of the cage but placed on 'house arrest'. During this time, he insisted on sleeping in our room at night and, as soon as dawn broke, devised many different methods of rudely awakening us.

Among his favourite tortures were: swinging on the curtains; nipping toes that strayed outside the duvet; dragging the bedside rug around the room; attacking the electric flexes and the telephone wire.

His most spectacular stunt, however, was the morning he landed in a great belly-flop right on Terry's face. Terry's terrified cries woke me just as violently as Murphy had woken him. It was a very long while before our pounding heart-rates finally subsided.

Murphy, of course, just sat on a bedside chair grinning. He knew we would forgive him anything because it was so good to see him being naughty after being so very poorly.

Fay Downs

Gone scrumping

We adopted two cats from the Cats Protection League – a small black mum, whom we called Ckei, and her handsome black-and-white son, whom we called Ptolemy – Jolly for short.

It soon became obvious that Jolly was disabled, having sustained an injury that left him with a weak back. In spite of this he was determined to go hunting and bring home trophies.

Obviously not quick enough for birds and mice, he

took to bringing home large juicy worms, which he laid on the carpet in front of the fire. Having been discouraged from doing this, he then found consolation in another hobby which continued for many years. He went scrumping. The apples he brought home were never windfalls – they were perfect, had been carefully 'picked'.

He carried home his trophies so proudly, each apple punctured by four tiny holes where he had gripped it in his mouth. Sometimes he carried them so tightly, he had to sit down and use his front paw to lever the apple from his teeth.

One day, he was caught in the act. 'Come quickly,' a newly moved-in neighbour was overheard calling to his wife, 'next-door's cat is walking across our garden with one of *our* apples in his mouth'.

As Jolly became older, his disability began to limit his scrumping activities. He still managed to visit neighbouring gardens, but often found himself unable to get back into our garden. Unperturbed, he would sit patiently waiting until somebody spotted him and passed him back over the wall.

Wendy Johnson

Squeaks, Squawks, He-haws and Thumpers

What a nerve!

We are thinking of changing the name of our house to 'The Seagulls' Café' because, all through the summer, when we open our front door, the following happens.

After the seagulls have eaten our cats' food, the one that nine out of ten cats prefer, they walk across the lawn and wash their beaks in the bird-bath. One particular gull is so tame that he often walks right into the house, even when our five moggies are around, and eats the food off a saucer. Got to give him ten out of ten for nerve!

Mrs Joan Rowland

Road hog!

During the war my sister, then aged seventeen, and advised to have an outdoor job, became a milk-lady. This entailed getting up very early, of course, travelling to the milk-bottle loading point and getting her horse and cart. She had various horses to cope with over the years, but one in particular was named Gabby. He had the knack of disappearing while she was delivering the milk, and she would find him with his head in the pig-bins which were placed at various lamp-posts in the roads at that time. He would knock the lids off and, despite having just had his breakfast, would search out tasty morsels. A certain lady was also in the habit of putting out crusts of bread for him and he would refuse to budge from her gatepost until he had a tit-bit. That was fine when she remembered, but . . .

His other 'trick' was when my sister took him into Bristol to be re-shod. He always knew when they were on their way home and used to go 'like the clappers' all through the main roads. The lights on the cart were two candles, one placed each side, in jam-jar-like containers. The roads, fortunately for my sister and Gabby, were not so busy in those days.

Peggy Kieser

Humps and bumps in the night

While on a touring holiday, my husband and I stayed overnight in a farmhouse near Hereford. While my husband was in the bathroom I turned back the bed covers and, horror of horrors, three *enormous* black spiders scuttled out from a pillow sham. Frozen to the spot – as, indeed, were the spiders now on the bed cover – my husband eventually responded to my screams, grabbed an empty glass, and, in the time-honoured way, shook them, one by one, out of the window. Having also responded to my insistence that he strip the bed right down to the ticking, and then remake it, he fell exhausted into bed and persuaded me to undress and do likewise. As I stood trembling nervously in my nightie, we heard our hosts come to bed in the next room. Precisely at that moment I glanced down at the replaced, pleated, floor-length bed valance

and let out a strangled scream as my worst fears were confirmed and I saw four – yes *four* – more enormous black hairy spiders.

'Good grief! Not more?' my exhausted husband cried out.

'More. *More*.' I hissed breathlessly back.

After further humping-thumping-bumping of bed linen and furniture during the second bout of bed-stripping, pillow-plumping, window-opening and shutting, and plus '*more-more*' breathless shrieks from me as another spider made a bid for freedom, plus evermore exhausted despairing cries from my husband, he finally went to sleep while I sat up all night with the light on.

The next morning, despite our age (late fifties) it was only too clear that our hosts thought we had been on some kind of erotic escapade, and, needless to say, they carefully avoided asking us if we had slept well! Thank God, we had only booked in for one night.

Kathryn Harper

Putting your foot in it

I had just had my kitchen re-done and was so pleased with the effect that I decided rather rashly that I would keep the surfaces totally clear. One morning I went shopping and, at the baker's, treated myself to a very large luscious strawberry-and-fresh-cream tart. I carried it home very carefully and put it gently next to the cooker, savouring the moment when I could eat it. But, as the washing machine had just finished, I took the clothes outside and hung them on the line. Unfortunately I had left the kitchen door open and when I got back all our hens were in the kitchen, and one was actually sitting in the sink! I pushed her out, but instead of just flying down she ran all the way round the beautifully cleaned U-shaped surfaces and, with the last step, put her foot right in the middle of my lovely cream cake!

Fortunately, my daughter's friend had a Saturday job in the bakery and the story made them laugh so much they sent me four more tarts.

Glennis Williams

Dog training

When Cockie, a cockatiel, first arrived our two dogs occasionally gave him a problem, but there was no doubt Cockie was 'top dog'. It sounded funny telling Cockie to leave a Labrador and a Collie-Cross alone. Then along came Ben, a two-year-old English Springer Spaniel, trained a little as a gun-dog. Try as he did, Cockie just could not make Ben toe-the-line like the other dogs.

One day Cockie was perched on the back of a chair cleaning himself when, with one leap, soon accompanied by much muffled squawking, Ben nabbed him, standing with Cockie's wings flapping from the side of his mouth. A sharp shout made him open his mouth and out came Cockie. Did Cockie panic? *No*! He hovered for a moment, then stuck his beak into Ben's nose before returning to the back of the chair to continue his ablutions as if nothing had happened.

Needless to say Ben (now eleven years) has had a lot of respect for Cockie since then.

Phil and Ann Barnes

Show me the way to go home . . .

We lived in a house with small willow-type trees around the gardens (sorry, I'm hopeless with names). The leaves were getting very diseased, so we decided to cut the trees down. At that time we also made wine and had a very good wheat-wine fermenting. After we drained the wine off, we always put the waste on the 'heap' at the bottom of the garden.

The birds loved our trees, but they also loved the drained-off wheat! And, on this occasion, we had cut the trees down . . . So, there were all these drunken birds swooping and dive-bombing around with nowhere to land. It was the funniest sight I had seen – poor, drunken, bewildered birds staggering around looking for their usual perches.

Mrs Joan Penman

Bird bar – open

Many years ago, when we were first married, we used to make a lot of our own wines using fresh fruit, berries or flowers. After fermenting the 'must' for many days in a plastic dustbin bought specially for wine-making purposes, the seething bubbling mass had to be strained ready for racking into demi-johns, and the remaining fruit pulp disposed of. My husband then had the bright idea of putting a panful of fat juicy raisins on to his compost heap. Big mistake!

The garden was soon full of birds, all fighting for a place at the bar, swooping off in all directions, colliding in mid-air, hanging grimly on to the fence, falling from branches etc. The cat watched all this in amazement, but left the scene very suddenly when a drunken starling literally ran across the grass towards him squawking what we took to be 'Put 'em up, puddycat'.

It was a scene of complete mayhem and debauchery, and it was a very long time before the cat was able to look a bird in the eye again.

Kath Worts

SK: Wonderful picture, Kath. Any raisins left?

CORY 95

Terrible Pets

Get me out of here!

Maureen, a girl I work with, had been to the Animal Refuge and selected Tess, an Alsatian, about a year old. Tess lives in a kennel outside, but is allowed in the house when the family is at home.

Already living at the house is Oz, the hamster, who somehow got out of his cage. Maureen, frantic, because her son, Andrew, would soon be home, was searching high and low. All of a sudden, as she was searching, the dog started to throw up. Maureen put Tess outside and was about to clean up the mess when the mess moved!

'Oh quick, Mike,' Maureen yelled, realizing what had happened. 'It's Oz. Put the poor thing out of its misery.'

Oz must have heard this because, when he moved again, he ran across the floor. By the time Maureen had caught him he was reasonably clean, but not very sweet-smelling!

Well, it's four days later now, and Oz, fed-and-watered, in his new abode well out of Tess's way, seems none the worse for his ordeal. Maureen thinks he must have been inside Tess for at least five minutes, and we are all amazed that he is alive and well.

Lyn Charlton

The service is terrible here!

Grandma was sitting in the sunroom waiting for her breakfast, with Judy, our Trinidad parrot, keeping her company. Maybe I was a little late attending to them, but as I came through with the breakfast tray, Judy enunciated very clearly 'Ah fed up, you know. Ah fed up'.

Mrs J. W. Young

Drama queens!

A member of our animal-mad household is Sydney, a parrot, who used to send Muppet, our Jack Russell, into complete hysteria by first of all mewing at her like a cat, barking at her in her own bark, and finally throwing seed out of his bowl over her head.

Is it any wonder she didn't like birds.

Terry Moule

Operation ele

A baby elephant visited the Equine Clinic at the Animal Health Trust to make use of our X-ray machine – one of the most powerful in Europe. The Trust is designed for horses not elephants and, as the baby elephant was too

large to fit into any of the stables, his bed for the night was one of our large, roomy, padded anaesthetic boxes. He quickly settled down, but as he was to have an operation the next day he had not been fed and woke up very hungry in the small hours of the morning.

In his quest for food he managed to force open the doors of the anaesthetic box and get into the operating theatre. He had a whale of a time exploring before his crashing around alerted the duty vet. Anyone who says bulls in china shops cause damage, should see the effects of an elephant in an operating theatre!

Phil Spiby

Who am I?

My two daughters, when young, had a rabbit. One does not think of rabbits as being particularly entertaining, but Bungey was quite a character.

During the summer he used to entertain his friends – mostly sparrows and the odd robin – to tea in his hutch; they would pop in through the wire-mesh at the front and peck about among the cereal and seeds while he sat watching benignly.

On cold winter nights, however, he had a box in the corner of the kitchen and it was then that his true character emerged – Bungey thought he was a dog! His favourite trick was to hop around the kitchen picking up stray shoes (even wooden exercise sandals) one at a time in his mouth and taking them back to his box, where he would pile up his trophies, looking very pleased with himself. Fluffy slippers sent him into a frenzy – we think he thought they

were lady rabbits – and anyone wearing them could find a loudly grunting passionate (oh, *yes*, they *do*) rabbit clinging lovingly to their foot.

At breakfast time, as soon as he smelt toast cooking, he would sit up very straight in his box, ears erect, and everyone, including visitors, would be expected to contribute a finger of toast. Bungey would 'beg' on his haunches like a dog, snatch the toast before you could change your mind, then, turning his back on you, crunch it ecstatically.

He enjoyed the company of other animals, although he was *not* too keen on having his ears washed by one of my daughter's cats, and was often to be seen sitting with his front paws resting on a recumbent dog.

Jacky Lewis

SK: I particularly like Bungey's attitude to life!

A wing and a prayer!

We had been looking after my in-laws' Orange Canary who had never sung since the day they bought it. My daughter was changing his drinking water when the canary escaped and headed for the open patio doors. As it went to fly outside, Buster, our Cocker Spaniel, leapt up and caught it in his mouth. I looked out into the garden and saw Buster running around the garden with the head of the bird sticking out of his mouth. I set off in pursuit.

Finally Buster ran back indoors, went under the dining-room table and deposited the bird on the carpet. Although it was still breathing I did not expect it to last long. I placed it back in the cage and we all went off to Church. We came home expecting the canary to be feet upwards at the bottom of the cage, but no! It was sitting on its perch singing away for all it was worth.

Vincent Carrington

SK: Bit of excitement does a bird good.

I like it here!

When our son Philip was three years old my then husband and I rescued a donkey foal that was being neglected and in need of some tender loving care. He was only about eight weeks old with small body, long gangly legs and enormous ears, so we called him Dillan after the rabbit on *Magic Roundabout*.

We fenced off half our garden to give him a nice paddock and built him a cedar wood stable. An ideal pet for Philip to grow up with, we thought! Our house has a

small lane up one side and the local children regularly called in to see Dillan on their way home from school, bringing him peppermints and apples. Thus began the creation of a *very* spoiled donkey. His first year with us was one of drought, and hay was pretty scarce. Now donkeys are supposed to be excellent for clearing rough grazing and eating thistle hay, so say the books, but *not* Dillan. We got so worried about his refusal to eat what the book said he would eat that we went to beg a local race-horse breeder to sell us his best hay!

We also bought a head-collar to take him out for walks, but Dillan's favourite activity was to drop his head and bite you on the thigh, and while you hopped on one leg in excruciating pain, he would then make a bid for freedom and bolt for it. Although he was only young he was very strong and it always took a few hundred yards to get him back under control.

He loved human company so when we were out gardening we let him out of his paddock to join us. One day, while we were otherwise engaged in the garden, he went missing. We searched everywhere. Thinking someone had left a garden gate open we even searched the streets, but no Dillan. It was only when I was walking disconsolately up the drive towards the house that I caught sight of him. He was standing in the lounge watching the television, which Philip had left on.

Lydia Skinner

Hear-hear

My daughters, Sarah and Becki, then aged about four and two, had two pet snails and were playing 'Snail Races' in the garden. 'Ready, steady, go,' shouted Becki to the snails. After a slight pause – and obviously disappointing results – Sarah said: 'Becki, your snail's *deaf*. He didn't hear you say, "Go".'

Jenni Beddington

What's your problem!

One Saturday evening I was happily absorbed in a book when the sound of a sheep bleating appeared closer and louder than usual. On looking out into the garden I saw that one of the sheep had jumped the field fence and was in the actual 'run', panicking that she couldn't get back to her 'pals'.

I went out into the garden and began running parallel to the run to encourage her to return to the field. On seeing me, she panicked all the more and hared off down the run, bleating at full volume. Nothing for it, I thought, so donning a pair of green wellies and grabbing a walking stick I duly clambered over my fence (4 ft) and endeavoured to shoo her back while attempting, semaphore-fashion, to attract the attention of the farmer. I had no idea sheep could jump so high, but, like a steeplechaser, she vaulted over the connecting fences in the run. Then, realizing she could not get back into the field that way, she turned around and headed back towards me at a rate of knots hitting me squarely in the lower regions of my body. Up – and over her – I went, landing flat on my face in a clump of nettles but still clutching my stick. It was only then that I realized that she would get to a dead-end, and be forced to turn around and head back again. Not wanting to be trampled over – and receive hoof-marks all over my back and head – I managed to jump up (I'm just out of my early forties) only to see her heading straight for me once again . . .

Where to go, I wondered? Two choices – the nettles again or the barbed-wire field fence. By this time my adversary had decided not to tangle with this person, clutching a stick, and had pushed herself through my fence and into my garden. Gotcha I thought . . . But now I had to surmount the four-foot garden fence again, complete with stick. By this time the pain had reached my brain,

but the sight of this manic sheep charging around my garden spurred me on. With considerable effort, I clambered over the fence suffering still more damage to lower portions of my body – thighs this time! Once over, and brandishing my stick at head height, I proceeded to chase the sheep through the flower beds, bobbing her with my stick whenever I got close enough and muttering 'Come here you, little bugger'. My neighbours' dog, spying the stick moving backwards and forwards, decided to join in, chasing along her side of the fence and barking furiously.

Fortunately, the end was in sight ... My adversary

decided to return to the run, through my fence, and head once more for her 'pals'. I continued to pursue 'her', climbing my fence yet again . . . only to see that, seemingly totally unaware of the chaos she had caused, she had finally managed to clamber back into the field and was calmly chewing grass with the rest of the flock.

By this time, I was in a state of complete collapse, but I still had to clamber back over the fence and get indoors without injuring myself further. Needless to say, it was not until I slid (gently) into the bath that I could see the funny side.

Ms Margaret Green

Where am I?

A friend of mine had a very old British Bulldog with
heavy jowls, called (naturally enough at the time) Winston.
Although looking formidable and fearsome, Winston was
in fact as soft as a kitten. She also had a budgie that was
allowed out of his cage to fly around the living-room.

One day we were sitting chatting while Winston lay
in his usual position in front of the fire, peacefully dozing.
The budgie was enjoying his trip around the room, but
then decided to land an inch or two in front of Winston's
nose – bobbing his head to and fro as budgerigars do.
Suddenly, Winston's mouth opened and snapped the
budgie up whole!

Before any of us could move, a bulge appeared in Winston's cheek, then first a head, and then the rest of the
budgie hopped out. He ruffled his feathers and, somewhat
shaken, flew back to the safety of his cage. Winston dozed
on.

Alan Pettit

A Mars a day . . .

Rosetta, a wonderful pedigree Ayrshire cow, had a tre-
mendous affectionate affinity with four schoolboys, who
loved throwing their arms around their dark-eyed beauty
of the cow-shed. Her nickname quickly became
'Cuddles'. 'She's such a loving cow,' said one lad with
innocent sincerity.

With the passage of time, the love-affair deepened, and
Rosetta's affections grew stronger, particularly when the
lads discovered that the way to her heart was through her

stomach. 'Wonder if Cuddles would like a bit of my Mars bar,' said one. The unexpected gesture was greeted even more unexpectedly by a rough outstretched tongue snaffling the prize. 'Blimey! She's eaten it!' he gasped.

After this, Cuddle's diet of Mars bars increased daily, with each lad – Colin, Peter, John and Michael – contributing a titbit each every day – and she went absolutely crazy whenever she heard the sound of the Mars bar wrapping paper.

Eventually, a letter was written to Mars bars' manufacturers, telling of Rosetta's obsession – and her magnificent performances in devouring the product. The reply, however, was negative, saying that a cow had already been selected for the Galaxy advertisement. The lads thought this disgraceful, because (to quote their words) 'That cow only moos – our Cuddles *eats* it!'

Rosetta continued to claim a very special place in all our hearts, and we were particularly touched when her milk-yield fell, while she sulked for days whenever the schoolboys went back to school. She lived a long life on the farm – a life which, I am sure, was enriched by the exchange of affection with the boys – and, not least, her 'galloping consumption' of Mars bars!

Gordon Currie

Do come again!

During the war when my mum and I were living in Devon, I stayed with a family whose aged aunt came to stay for the weekend and brought her Macaw with her. It spent more time out of its huge cage than in it, usually sitting on top and pecking at anyone who came near enough. One afternoon it grabbed at – and caught – one of my pigtails, and climbed on to my head. I screamed, it screamed, and everyone else fell about laughing. The wretched bird then did a 'whoopsie' down my neck. That increased my screaming and the parrot's falsetto, and the laughter. I would have happily strangled it if I could, and I've hated parrots ever since!

Frances

Swanning about

Walking along the sea-front between Clacton and Walton-on-Naze last summer with my sister-in-law we spotted a swan just out at sea. We always think of swans as stately birds, but this one had a sense of humour. It was surfing! It was swimming out several yards then turning and letting the waves carry it back to shore. It would then walk a few feet up the beach, turn round and do the same again.

Mrs Peggy Fairhall

Stage Door Johnny

We have a smallholding and keep mostly rescued animals – battery hens, goats, donkeys, cats, rabbits and Toby, my horse, who isn't a rescue.

About two years ago we got our first rabbits, sisters, Dilly and Doris. They live in a converted chicken ark with a series of runs connected by tunnels. Good DIY I thought. Not long after their arrival, we noticed 'Stage Door Johnny', a wild rabbit who would be in attendance outside the ark, morning, noon and night.

One Saturday morning I looked out of the kitchen window and noticed Dilly and Doris grazing on the bank. One of their tunnels had obviously come out of a run (not such good DIY after all). I called Carolyn who rushed downstairs with a blanket to catch them, but no such luck. On sight of the blanket the rabbits hopped either side of it. By this time the other animals were all making so much noise for their breakfast that Carolyn left Dilly and Doris to feed the others. Then, as usual, she put Dilly and Doris's food in their hutch and, to our amazement, they hopped back in allowing the door to be quickly shut behind them.

A few weeks later, Carolyn opened up Dilly and Doris's hutch and saw some straw moving in a strange fashion. Underneath the straw she found eleven baby rabbits. So,

Dilly and Doris had obviously been out for a bit longer than we thought, and this was definitely a case of 'breed like rabbits'. Needless to say we haven't seen much of Johnny lately, but when we do . . .

Worried of Waldron

Wrong prayer

Edward was very upset when his pet hen, Hetty, was killed by a fox. When he arrived at school, his teacher could see that he was wretched, and listened sympathetically as he mumbled his hen had died. She then obviously had a word with the headmistress because, at Assembly, the Head said: 'Now children, we will all say a prayer for Edward because his Nan has died.'

An indignant voice called out from the back of the hall: 'Not my Nan, my *hen*'.

Phyllis Brown

A tail story

My friend was a farmer's wife and her son, about four at the time, loved running round watching – and making friends with – the animals. One day he came rocketing in through the kitchen door shouting: 'Mummy, mummy. Come quick. Jimmy [the cattleman] is having a *terrible* time. There's a cow lying down, and a calf is trying to climb up its bottom, and Jimmy can't pull it out . . .'

Duncan Stewart

Walking the frog

We came across 'Spice', our tabby cat, playing with something in the garden. The 'something' turned out to be a frog, and, despite being mauled by Spice, it was still alive. We do not have a pond, but our neighbour does, so we decided she must be the frog's owner. We put a little water in a bucket, put the poor creature in the water, and set off to our neighbour. 'Oh no,' she said, on our arrival, 'we don't like frogs and we don't have any in our pond.'

The only answer was to take him to the brook about half-a-mile from our house. Normally when we take a walk into the countryside we don't see any other humans, just foxes, deer, cats . . . But, of course, the day we set out carrying a large black bucket, with a frog inside, was the day we met quite a few people out enjoying their Sunday. One woman jogged past, staring at our bucket. 'It's a frog,' my husband said conversationally. 'Oh yes,' she replied, jogging on, 'lots of people take their frogs out for a walk.'

We called our frog Felix, as it was so nearly cat food!
Helena and Jeremy Minton

What a clever bunny am I

Several years ago we bought my eldest stepson a dwarf rabbit for his birthday, but the novelty soon wore off and he became my pet.

Our garden is not very large, mainly lawn with flower-beds around the sides. Whenever we could, we let the rabbit have the freedom of the garden and the resulting destruction of the plants was compensated for by the delightful playfulness of this little animal enjoying his freedom.

In time the rabbit became familiar with everything in the garden, and he would follow my husband around with eager curiosity whenever he was gardening.

One year my husband was busy planting daffodil bulbs, and, as usual, the rabbit was following him around. After much hard back-breaking work, my husband came in for a cup of tea.

After a while we both went out into the garden only to find . . . all the daffodil bulbs lined up along the path, and one very smug-looking bunny standing nearby.

No, he didn't end up as rabbit pie and was sorely missed when he died in 1993. We have since taken in another rabbit from the RSPCA and are constantly surprised by the 'intelligence' and 'humour' of these delightful creatures.

Mrs Avril J. Hale

Close aftershave!

We were on holiday, staying with friends in the USA. One morning, on hearing a commotion outside, I looked out of the bedroom window to see a skunk with a marmalade jar stuck on its head, followed by the Basset Hound from next door, followed by my small son Blyth, followed by my husband John.

Every so often the skunk would stop and so would everyone else, while it tried to remove the jar with its front paws. Then the procession would move off again. My husband, who is the world's greatest animal lover, decided he could not let the skunk's agony go on a moment longer and took his life in his hands, picking up the skunk in one hand and pulling at the jar with the other. Almost with a pop, the jar came off. The skunk looked very bewildered, and, as John put it down, it immediately turned its tail towards him. Shock! Horror! However, the poor skunk must have been 'all sprayed out' because nothing happened and he shuffled off followed by the Basset Hound.

When we told our American friends about this incident, they said they would not have done that for anything. It is the *worst* smell in the world and takes ages to remove. We suspect the skunk had been raiding the garbage and that the jar had been stuck on his head for quite a time, as he was quite thin. Without John's heroism the poor thing would have starved to death.

Diana Louis

Manners maketh . . .

Basil is a blue-and-gold Macaw who came to us rather oven-ready because of his habitual feather plucking (little dear!). His disgusting habits apart from feather-plucking include:

saying 'Thank you' and asking 'Is that nice?' as soon as anyone in the room has something to eat. His comments get louder and more pointed until he is given a piece to try;

nibbling the chocolate off biscuits and spitting the rest on the floor;

sitting on my husband's shoulder to share a bowl of porridge, and then wiping his beak on his collar (my husband's collar, not Basil's, you understand);

screaming 'Mum, help!' whenever he is ignored. (I hope there are no NSPCC inspectors within earshot – could be very embarrassing);

sitting on the threshold of his cage spitting sunflower seed husks on to the head of the poor mug cleaning up the debris beneath;

insisting on sharing cups of tea, which involves sticking his whole head in the cup, often talking with a beak full of tea, and then making disgusting snorkelling noises as he swallows;

biting the ends of grapes and sucking the insides out, again with stomach-curdling sound effects.

Altogether, a charming fellow our Basil!

Anon of Hants

How do you like your eggs?

Having a suitable outhouse and fairly extensive grounds, my wife, Sylvia, decided that she would like to have a few hens wandering around the place. I duly set up a roosting shelf and nest-boxes, and we obtained a handsome cockerel and half-a-dozen hens. In due course, laying commenced and we had a regular supply of fresh free-range eggs. After a time, however, laying dropped off, and we assumed that this was natural.

One day, as I was working in a patch set aside for the bonfire and compost heap, I caught sight of a movement out of the corner of my eye. Turning I saw one of the hens, Flossie by name and always slightly wayward, emerge from under a sheet of back polythene. Curious, I lifted the sheet and found a neat hollow containing sixteen eggs!

It was now that the dilemma arose. How long does an egg stay fresh? Which were the first and last eggs to be laid? After some discussion we decided that they would all have to be broken before use and, for a week, we lived on scrambled eggs, omelettes, soufflés, egg-custards etc.

Ever since then we have kept a careful eye on Flossie, but occasionally the cry goes up 'Where is Flossie?' and a search ensues to discover her new hiding places!

Raymond Elliott

Strolling . . . just strolling

My pony, Misty, a pretty grey Welsh mountain pony, was truly one of the family. Each night he was carefully locked in his field, but every night he would somehow succeed in getting out and would stroll contentedly around our village always ending up at dawn sitting among the graves in the churchyard amusing the Vicar's wife. One day he was spotted window-shopping, peering into the Co-op window. He lived to a grand old age of twenty-six, eventually dying of a stroke, and my poor father had to bury him with the help of a digger in the churchyard he loved so much.

Jenny

Smoke gets in your eyes

Our son, Richard, then aged about five, had a small hamster called Hammy. Unfortunately the hamster, an adventurer, was never happy in his beautiful cosy cage and was forever escaping – especially at night which gave him a head start. Once he was missing for several days before being discovered in the tray under my gas cooker.

On another occasion, as we sat having our meal, we heard strange scratching noises overhead and realized he had gone off again. The bedroom was thoroughly investigated, but no Hammy was found. Then a small hole was discovered in the floorboards under a wardrobe and we could hear Hammy running backwards and forwards, limited only in his journeys by a joist beam which restricted him to one corner area of his underfloor kingdom.

Nothing could persuade him to come out and much frustration and a few youthful tears followed. Eventually the family retired downstairs leaving Dad to solve the problem.

We returned some time later to find the carpet rolled

CARY 95.

back, the wardrobe moved, one floorboard removed and Dad sitting cross-legged on the floor.

He was puffing away at his pipe and blowing the resulting smoke down a small rubber tube into the space under the floorboards.

Shortly afterwards, amidst much laughter from us, a coughing, bewildered Hammy emerged and gave himself up. He lived a long time afterwards, but gave up adventuring!

Mrs Jean Earle

They came to stay!

My daughter is an animal lover. No matter how many legs it has, it is cherished. After stick-insects had escaped in the house, I thought a few small caterpillars would be easy to control. What was I thinking?

They grew rapidly into huge, green, active caterpillars that ate avidly. In fact, we must be the first people to take our caterpillars on holiday with us as our pet-sitter could not be persuaded to cope with their twice-daily feedings. They only ate May leaves, and there was only one bush in a five-mile radius of our holiday home. I had to sneak out before sunrise to chop lumps off, and, after a few days, the bush looked rather pruned!

Then suddenly they stopped eating and built themselves huge cocoons. I must admit I found this stage rather moving. What on earth made them stop eating, seek a suitable twig, and entomb themselves? We put the aquarium they lived in up on a high shelf and forgot about them. They were supposed to hatch out the following year. The cat drew our attention to rustling some weeks later. On checking we found an enormous green Indian Moon Moth struggling to unfold its wings.

We put sticks for them to hang on to as their wings gradually unfurled. We were all mesmerized as they crawled out of the cocoons, and pumped their wings up.

We had twelve in the end – some male and some female. The tail streamers were different on each of the sexes. Then the next major problem. They have no mouth parts, and only live a week until they mate, lay eggs and die. Well, we gave the room over to them – after all it was only for a week.

They flew up and drifted down in the evenings, and spent the days on the curtains and picture rails. If you have never watched TV half in the dark with huge Moon Moths drifting past, you don't know what you are missing!

They lived for weeks! We collected eggs from all over the room, but none of them subsequently hatched. One part of me regrets this, but it is nice to get the room back and not to have to keep the cat out, not to have to carefully vacuum clean where they are not, or count them to make sure that one was not caught in a cobweb, etc., etc.

Mrs Joyce Clayton

One good turn deserves . . .

Many years ago I had a pet rabbit who, during the winter, used to sit in the conservatory and, as a special treat, was allowed to take a turn around the sitting-room.

Having put him back in his cage one night, I went to turn the lights on. Noticing that a bulb needed changing in the standard lamp situated at one end of the settee, I changed the bulb. But there was still no light. I then checked the plug and wires at the other end of the settee – all were okay. I then changed the fuse, just in case. Still no light. Thinking this was a problem best left to the weekend, I gave up. It was not until I was moving the settee to retrieve the dog's ball that I found that the rabbit had neatly chewed through the wires!

How he lived to tell the tale I do not know, but he did – eventually escaping from his cage to find his own Bright Eyes.

Jenny Kendrew

Holidays – who needs them!

It is quite easy to get trapped where we live, especially during the holiday season. If you want to escape for a holiday somewhere, it is nearly always necessary to book a ferry.

We – me, my husband, three children, plus dog – were booked on the 8.00 a.m. ferry, having arranged to leave the rest of our menagerie in the care of a good capable friend.

Up at the crack of dawn, I mucked out Penny Pony, the mare, and her young foal, while middle son sat on fence sucking a straw and hubby wandered around, muttering on about having to load the car all by himself. Mare and foal were at last in the adjoining paddock when I (still in the stable) heard a terrific crash. I rushed out – Hubby was there, son was there, Penny Pony was there – the foal was not!

'Where is it? Where is it?' I screamed frantically.

'In the ditch,' son replied casually. 'She whizzed round a bit, then took off over the hedge, and landed in the ditch.'

Needless to say, although it is about a 5ft drop, I did the same. The foal was remarkably calm really and her mother wasn't in the least perturbed. Obliging as ever, Hubby went off to get a saw to remove part of the hedge. Then, this achieved, he pulled, I pushed, and out popped the foal none the worse for her escapade. Her name? Whizzy, of course.

That, however, was not the end of our pre-travel dramas. I also keep a couple of sheep. It was nearing 7.00 a.m. (8 o'clock ferry remember!) and I went off to check them. My husband, by this time, was irritated about having to change his clothes after rescuing the foal. I went into the field; the weather had taken a turn for the worse and it was a bit wet and windy. As I looked around, I couldn't believe my eyes. One of the sheep had produced a lamb – a pathetic creature too cold and too weak to stand and suckle. I rubbed it, dried it, and rushed back home to tell the family. By now it was 7.20.

'If we are not at the ferry terminal half an hour before it goes, we run the risk of losing our booking. Honestly, if we're not on the 8.00 ferry I shall . . .' muttered my normally placid husband.

Oh boy, was I in a fix! What a dilemma. It was 7.25 and here I was still covered in undergrowth, afterbirth, and other indescribable animal smells, with my husband threatening all manner of things – which clearly added up to a choice between him and the ailing lamb!

Well, he is rather a dear, does put up with a lot, and we have been married a very long time.

We finally caught the ferry with three minutes to spare. Whizzy was none the worse for her adventure, and the lamb – with a lot of TLC while we were away – survived to be strong and healthy.

Penny Green

Left, right, left right

In the garden we keep an old washing-up bowl under which we keep a tin of food for feeding the cat in the morning.

One morning, about 2 a.m., we were woken by a strange scraping noise, and thought it was probably roaming cats trying to get at the food under the bowl. We tried to return to sleep but the strange noise persisted and, eventually overcome by curiosity, we went to see what was happening. On opening the back door, the bowl, to our utter astonishment, was trotting down the garden path at a fair rate of knots. Not being the sort who enjoys unpleasant surprises I told my husband to see what was happening. Very slowly he lifted the bowl and there, underneath, was one of the biggest hedgehogs I have ever seen with a tin of cat food stuck on his head!

We took the tin off and let him go, which he did very rapidly. Now, we put him his own saucer of food out at night, but we will never forget the sight of that bowl trotting off down the garden path.

Mrs Joan Hodskinson

THE END!

Acknowledgements

Special thanks are due to:

Sarah Kennedy's BBC Radio 2 *Dawn Patrol* programme who have given permission for their letters and poems to be included in this book; Christine Gordon-Jones of Cobra & Bellamy for allowing us to use her puppies and cat, Burma, for the cover; Heather Cary for her cartoons; and David Ward for taking the cover photographs.

The Publishers have made every effort to contact the contributors to this book. Should she have failed to do so, she will be pleased to correct this, after notification, at the earliest possible opportunity.

A royalty of 4 per cent of the retail price of this book will be paid to the PDSA (People's Dispensary for Sick Animals) on every copy sold.

A SELECTION OF BOOKS FROM BBC/PENGUIN

BBC (Penguin logo)

Great Railway Journeys
Photographs by Tom Owen Edmunds

Against all the odds – despite the aeroplane and the motor car – trains are still the best way to travel to discover a country. In *Great Railway Journeys* six travellers write about their railway journeys through terrain for which they have a particular attachment, curiosity and affection.

Mark Tully takes the Khyber Mail from Karachi to the breathtaking Khyber Pass; Clive Anderson explores the route from Hong Kong to Mongolia; Natalia Makarova journeys through her Russian past, from St Petersburg to Tashkent.

Whether by steam or diesel, on cattle trucks, double-decker coaches or the luxury City Gold service, each of these journeys – as well as those undertaken by Lisa St Aubin de Terán, Rian Malan and Michael Palin – turns into an adventure.

Crusades Terry Jones and Alan Ereira

In 1095 Pope Urban II made an announcement that would change the world. He called upon Christians to march under the banner of the Cross and save their brothers in the East from the advance of Islam. This vision of crusading Christianity dominated the events of the next two centuries. With wit and humour, making the history of the Crusades accessible to all readers, Terry Jones and Alan Ereira bring vividly to life the compelling, often horrific, story of the fanatics and fantasists, knights and peasants, corrupt clergy and duplicitous leaders who were caught up in these fervent times.

A SELECTION OF BOOKS FROM BBC/PENGUIN

BBC ⊕

Who Learns Wins Phil Race
Positive Steps to the Enjoyment and Re-discovery of Learning

It's never too late to learn. School may have been dreary and left us with a low opinion of our abilities, but with *Who Learns Wins* it's never been easier to make a fresh start. In this stimulating book Phil Race demonstrates with humour and understanding that we are capable of far more than we ever thought possible. Whether we want to speak a new language, understand mathematics, assemble a piece of furniture or grow chrysanthemums, this invaluable book helps us to rediscover the thrill and excitement of learning.

In Search of the Dead Jeffrey Iverson
A Scientific Investigation of Evidence for Life after Death

What lies beyond death? For over a century scientists have searched for proof that we survive death. In this book, based on a BBC television documentary series, Jeffrey Iverson examines the evidence for this and other aspects of the paranormal through a fascinating variety of case studies.

In Search of the Dead calls for a greater understanding of the scientific framework for the paranormal, and convincingly argues that the future could see a new science of Mind. And though the ultimate reality of the universe remains a mystery at present, transcending death may be the next stage in the evolution of human consciousness.

A Guide to Parliament David Davis MP

Have you ever wondered why the Speaker has to be dragged to the Chair? Who is Black Rod? And what is a three-line whip? Combining amusing anecdotes with invaluable information, David Davis chronicles the history of Parliament, and illustrates how committees function and the roles of the Prime Minister, Cabinet and Departments of State, giving a fascinating insight into Britain's greatest institution.

A SELECTION OF BOOKS FROM BBC/PENGUIN

Greek as a Treat Peter France
An Introduction to the Classics

We can get through life nowadays without Greek. Yet, as Peter France argues, we are missing out on the best of it. Shakespeare, Byron, Shelley, Dr Johnson and Winston Churchill are unlikely all to have been wrong. In this exhilarating book Peter France opens our eyes to classical Greece and to the 'greats' – Homer, Pythagoras, Aeschylus, Socrates and Plato – ready and waiting to enrich our twentieth-century lives.

John Dunn's Answers Please

Amazing answers, fascinating facts, tantalizing trivia: *John Dunn's Answers Please*, from John Dunn's popular BBC Radio 2 programme, is a wonderfully entertaining compendium of general knowledge questions and answers. What is Amaretto made from? How much water is there in the world? Why do geese fly in a V-formation? Who was Big Bertha?

Arranged in A–Z order, *John Dunn's Answers Please* is a treasure trove of fact, information, detail and knowledge that will keep the whole family amused and entertained for hours.

A SELECTION OF BOOKS FROM BBC/PENGUIN

BBC (Penguin logo)

Great Journeys
Photographs by Tom Owen Edmunds

Here seven great travellers of our time rediscover some of the world's most spectacular and inhospitable terrain, tracing these remarkable journeys with idiosyncratic style and humour. Colin Thubron returns to the Silk Road; Naomi James sails amongst the Polynesian islands; Hugo Williams travels the Pan American Highway; Miles Kington uncovers the old Burma Road used by Chaing Kai-shek; Norman Stone follows the Viking route from the Baltic to the Black Sea; William Shawcross traces the Salt Road in the Sahara and Philip Jones Griffiths revisits the Ho Chi Minh Trail twenty-one years after photographing the Vietnam War.

Living Islam   Akbar S. Ahmed

Although there are around a billion Muslims in the world, most discussion of Islam is based on clichés or outright prejudice. This lively and compelling book sets out to bridge gulfs of misunderstanding. Going back to the sources of Islam, to the Prophet Muhammad and the Quran's 'five pillars', looking at Muslim communities from Samarkand to the Outer Hebrides, Akbar S. Ahmed explores the issues with insight and sympathy, penetrating beyond the stereotypes to the realities of Islamic life.

A SELECTION OF BOOKS FROM BBC/PENGUIN

BBC (Penguin logo)

Island Race John McCarthy and Sandi Toksvig

As a hostage in Beirut, John McCarthy had a dream of sailing on the bow of a classic yacht: to him it was a powerful vision of freedom. In *Island Race* he teams up with his old friend, comedian Sandi Toksvig, to fulfil the dream by sailing around the coast of Britain. In the beautiful *Hirta*, an eighty-year-old wooden cutter, they call in at nearly fifty ports and harbours, and encounter an enormous range of communities – from Buddhist monks on Holy Island in the north to the busy seaside resorts of England's south coast. In this warm-hearted book, by turns thoughtful and hilarious, the gutsy duo make a great many entertaining discoveries and offer two sometimes conflicting but complementary views of Britain from the sea.

The Making of Pride and Prejudice Sue Birtwistle and Susie Conklin

Filmed on location in Wiltshire and Derbyshire, *Pride and Prejudice*, with its lavish sets and distinguished cast, was watched and enjoyed by millions. Chronicling eighteen months of work – from the original concept to the first broadcast – *The Making of Pride and Prejudice* brings vividly to life the challenges and triumphs involved in every stage of production of this sumptuous television series.

Follow a typical day's filming, including the wholesale transformation of Lacock village into the minutely detailed setting of Jane Austen's Meryton. Discover how an actor approaches the character, how costumes and wigs are designed, and how the roles of casting directors, researchers, and even experts in period cookery and gardening, contribute to the series. Including many full-colour photographs, interviews and lavish illustrations, *The Making of Pride and Prejudice* is a fascinating insight into all aspects of a major television enterprise.

A SELECTION OF BOOKS FROM BBC/PENGUIN

BBC (Penguin logo)

The Death of Yugoslavia   Laura Silber and Allan Little

While the western world stood by, seemingly paralysed, and international peace efforts broke down, the former Yugoslavia was witnessing Europe's bloodiest conflict for half a century. *The Death of Yugoslavia* is the first account to go behind the public face of battle and into the closed worlds of the key players in the war. Laura Silber, Balkans correspondent for the *Financial Times*, and Allan Little, award-winning BBC journalist, plot the road to war and the war itself.

Drawing on eye-witness testimony, scrupulous research and hundreds of interviews, they give unprecedented access to the facts behind the media stories. Could anything have been done to prevent this terrible tragedy? What will be its lasting effects? The authors consider these questions and assess the present situation and its implications for future international relations.

States of Terror   Peter Taylor
Democracy and Political Violence

Terrorism is the scourge of most modern democracies, but how can governments fight back without adopting the same terrorist tactics and trampling on those human rights they claim to uphold? In this vivid and disturbing book, based on an acclaimed documentary series, Peter Taylor takes readers inside Irish Cabinet meetings and IRA courts martial. He examines the aims and methods of Palestinian radicals and their Mossad pursuers, and talks to the sons of assassinated enemies who may provide a glimmer of hope. His findings bring fresh insight into one of today's key moral and political issues.

A SELECTION OF BOOKS FROM BBC/PENGUIN

BBC (Penguin logo)

The Complete BBC Diet Dr Barry Lynch

If you enjoy food and dread the thought of dieting, think again. Now you can lose weight without the misery of hunger with *The Complete BBC Diet*. By reducing fat and sugar and increasing fibre you can transform your diet – and your figure – and keep weight off for good. Medically approved, easy to follow and tremendously successful, this book has helped hundreds of thousands of people become fitter and slimmer.

Body in Action Sarah Key
The Complete Self-Help Programme for Stiff Joints

Many people suffer from joint pain or stiffness at some time in their lives, whether it is tennis elbow or chronic arthritis. Much discomfort is preventable, however, and some conditions reversible, if we know how. This remarkable book demonstrates how to keep the back and limbs supple, what to do for particular joint problems, how to spot warning signs, which exercises to do to maintain suppleness and improve flexibility, and provides a general programme of preventative exercise.

With clearly illustrated instructions, *Body in Action* is a professional approach to improving your health and to looking and feeling younger every day.

A SELECTION OF BOOKS
FROM BBC/PENGUIN

BBC (●)

The Trotter Way to Millions
Based on the BBC Television series *Only Fools and Horses*

Whether it's selling fire-damaged woks or off-loading a collection of *haute couture* Bulgarian 3-piece suits, Derek 'Del Boy' Trotter, the *crème de la menthe* of Peckham's entrepreneurs, has a style that is uniquely his own.

A graduate of the School of Hard Knocks, the University of Life and, ultimately, the Peckham Business School, Del has now written the definitive 'how to' book for everyone who wants to operate at the sharp end of the financial pencil. As told to John Haselden, *The Trotter Way to Millions* guarantees by this time next year we'll all be millionaires! Lovely jubbly!

The Terrible Twos   Compiled by Sarah Kennedy
True Stories of Tots and Toddlers

Small children have a way with words. They can come out with innocent remarks that can make you squirm, roar with laughter or die of shame. Anyone who has ever spent a few hours with a lively child will have an idea of the fun in store in this collection of children's logic.

Now greatly expanded and revised, this new edition of *The Terrible Twos* contains the best of the real-life stories sent to Sarah Kennedy by listeners of her BBC Radio 2 programme, *Dawn Patrol*. Illustrated by some of Britain's top cartoonists, *The Terrible Twos* promises a royalty to BBC Children in Need, a registered charity, for every copy sold. So you can chuckle and help children's charities at the same time!